The Making
of a Suicide Bomber

By

David Stansfield

Malo mori quam foedari

The Making of a Suicide Bomber/
David Stansfield

ISBN-13: 9798727253960

**SULBY HALL
PUBLISHERS**

USA: PO Box 6867
Malibu CA 90264

Canada: 28 Duncannon Drive,
Toronto ON M5P 2M1

www.sulbyhall.com

Cover design by Neel Muller Studios

Printed in the
United States of America

ALSO BY DAVID STANSFIELD

FICTION
One Last Great Wickedness
The Man Who Murdered Time
Attack at Noon
Blood
Take Nothing For Granted
Highway Robbery
A Season of Monsters
Two Eyes For An Eye

NON-FICTION
Origins: A History of Canada
The Seventh Coming
ISIS: The Most Dangerous People On Earth
Islam vs. ISIS
Get The Hate Out Of America
Got a Couple of Minutes?
(221 500-word stories)
Free the Children!
(with Anthony Barton)

SHORT BOOKS ABOUT TERRORISM
1. ISIS Wants To Kill You
2. ISIS Wants Your Head
3. ISIS Goes Viral
4. Faces of Terror
5. Roots of Terror

Introduction ·

I wrote this little book not to try to excuse suicide bombers, but to try to explain them so that we can eventually eradicate them, literally tear them out by the roots. But first we have to find these roots so that we can study them and understand them as fully as we can.

Just as we will never be able to eliminate cancer until we understand what causes it, so we will never be able to eliminate terrorism until we understand its causes. We can build all the walls and armies and armaments in the world, but this is merely slapping on Band-Aids. We will never be truly safe until we destroy the root cause of the disease itself.

As the New York Times put it in a recent op-ed piece: "When people are born with the same human nature as you and I grow up to commit suicide bombings – or applaud them – there must be a reason. And it's at least conceivable their fanaticism is needlessly encouraged by American policy or rhetoric. Putting yourself in the shoes of people who do things you find abhorrent may be the hardest moral exercise there is. But it would be easier to excuse Americans who refuse to try if they didn't spend so much time indicting Islamic radicals for the same refusal. Somebody has to go first and if nobody does we're all in trouble."

So I am going to try to go first.

It's time to stop treating terrorism in a vacuum as if it's a general phenomenon that is simply evil and has just appeared out of nowhere for no good reason. Instead, if we're ever to find a cure for it we must look it in the face to see it for what it is: the product of a specific history and circumstance.

This is my attempt to put you, the reader, into the shoes of one particular people, some of whose members have been driven to such an extreme of pain and desperation they are prepared to do the unthinkable.

To achieve this, I have to get personal and particular and subjective myself for there are more than enough impersonal, general and objective books on the subject to sink a ship, all of them getting us precisely nowhere. So in order to help you identify with the particular people in question, I invite you first to identify with me.

This personal Odyssey proceeds through half a lifetime of experience with the Arab world that ends – well, but for the grace of God, it could well have ended very much as described here.

David Stansfield
Malibu CA
May 2021

Prologue

Like a fat black snake slithering down a rabbit hole, the convoy of armor-plated limousines squeezed through the moonlit village, the sides of the huge vehicles almost grazing the flint walls of the medieval shops and cottages that lined the narrow, meandering street.

Much to the relief of the line of fuming motorists trailing behind it, the convoy finally turned left at the twelfth-century Norman church whose brass memorial to a Crusader knight the villagers swore blind had once been "rubbed" by Lawrence of Arabia.

Moments later, the sombre procession plunged into a cathedral of elms and beeches, their branches interlaced against the sky like guardsmen crossing swords over a coffin. Then through a pair of towering gates to crunch across the gravel courtyard, finally purring to a halt in front of the exquisite Georgian manor.

The longest of the limos could have been taken for a hearse – if it hadn't been for the thicket of real life guardsmen that sprang up around it as if Burnham Wood had come once more to Dunsinane

As military helicopters rattled overhead and burly bodyguards in dark glasses and earpieces looked anxiously in all directions, the three men got out of the mammoth vehcle and mounted the flight of manor steps. One was young and lithe, the second old and obese, and the third so advanced in age he needed help from his companions to make the climb.

At the top of the steps, they turned for a moment to face the courtyard as if posing for posterity.

The Postcard

I had never seen anything like it. At the bottom of the postcard she'd just handed me before boarding the boat back to Morocco, below some rather sweet endearments in French, Jasmine had drawn a curious but strangely beautiful pattern of swirling lines and curlicues that danced up and down on my skin. The design was foreign and yet familiar, like an elaborate frieze that had been hovering around the edge of my consciousness as long as I could remember.

"It means I love you and I'm going to miss you terribly, *mon amour*," whispered Jasmine, nuzzling my neck.

"It's *writing*?"

"It's Arabic. My other language."

"Your other language? I didn't know you had another language. You come from French Morocco. You're French."

"I'm French and I'm Arab. I'm both."

"How do you do it?"

She took a pen and repeated the mysterious pattern, her hand moving across the card from right to left.

"But it's backwards. Mirror writing."

She smiled. "Didn't you know, David? 'Jasmine Through the Looking-Glass,' that's me."

"What's it sound like?"

She traced the undulations with her finger: "*Ana uhibbak wa sa-astafqidu lak kathiran ya habibi.*"

It was as if she'd run her finger down my back. If the writing was a painting, the reading was a song, the notes coming from deep inside her. The "q" was a kiss from the back of her throat. The strong "h" the hiss of a wave breaking on the beach, washing over me, the ocean breathing out her soul. This tiny, beautiful, dark-eyed girl, I'd always thought of as simply "French," had suddenly revealed another side of herself, another dimension.

I gazed into her face, at the dusky smudges round the eyes I loved to kiss. The French – and now Arab – bruises that never healed. Was I kissing them to make them better or to touch their darkness? There was more mystery here than I could fathom. She was a visitor from another planet who had exposed a subliminal glimmer of her true self. And behind that self another world, a parallel universe.

I remembered a BBC *Brains Trust* wireless program about how we can have a premonition of an event that hasn't happened yet, or conversely a *déjà vu* feeling about an event that is currently happening. One explanation was "Dunne's Time Theory": think of your life as an escalator, only there are many – perhaps an infinite number – of parallel escalators all out of sync with your own to varying degrees, either ahead or behind. Occasionally, it's possible to catch sight of one of these parallel escalators and see into another time dimension.

I was convinced that the parallel universe Jasmine had let me glimpse was of the *déjà vu* variety. She'd let me glimpse over my shoulder one of the neighboring escalators running slightly behind my own. It has always been there, an escalator I had ridden before, now a shadow in the corner of my eye like the smudges around her eyes. Waiting for me

I was bursting with questions: why had she never talked to me of this other life? What was this other world? How *could* you be both French and Arab at the same time?

The boat's foghorn sounded. She kissed me quickly, then ran up the gangplank to the Dover ferry and out of my life. Or so I thought.

Chapter One
Living In Palestine
1961

I loved you, so I drew these tides of men into my hands
and wrote my will across the sky in stars
To earn your Freedom, the seven-pillared worthy house
That your eyes might be shining for me
When they came.

– T.E. Lawrence

He is calm and I am also
He sips tea with lemon
and I drink coffee
This is the only thing that makes us different
I hum the melody of a song
He hums the melody of a song
I think: is he the mirror in which I see myself?
Then I look into his eyes but do not see him
And I leave the café in a hurry
I think: perhaps he is a killer or perhaps
he is a passerby who thought I was a killer

– Mahmoud
Darwish
Palestian poet

1

Jasmine. Of course. Of all the flowers the young man could have pressed into my hands as he showed me how to rub the white petals together in my palms, and then cup my hands to breathe in the sweet scent, it had to be Jasmine. It was the custom: different sensory modalities. Where I came from, they offered guests something to drink, here they offered you something to smell.

"This is your house, *ahlan wa sahlan*, welcome, welcome," said Ahmed, as he led me into the tiny one-story house, continuing to enunciate the lovely Arabic sounds slowly and clearly to make sure I understood every word.

Painstakingly, I had written out a want ad in my best classical Arabic explaining that I was a Cambridge University student studying the language and that to improve my command of its colloquial form I would like to spend the summer as a paying guest in an Arab family. I had then posted this ad to *al-Quds* – "The Holiness" – the leading Arabic newspaper in the city of that name, which foreigners knew as Jerusalem.

I'd received dozens of replies, all of them saying the same thing: "You are welcome to stay with our family for as long as you wish, but on one condition: that you promise faithfully never to pay for anything yourself. *Baituna huwa baituka,* our house is your house."

At university, there had been a lot of talk of this legendary Arab hospitality, but only now did it begin to sink in; another aspect of the strange new cultural landscape I'd ventured into the moment I stepped off the plane in Beirut a few days earlier. The blast of hot air that hit me had been like walking into an oven, but not a hostile Third World oven, more like a warm bath to soak away my British stiffness, to bring about some deep alchemical change in my bones as it drew me into another reality.

From the outset, I had resolved to speak exclusively in my halting Arabic. If anyone spoke to me in English, I'd respond, "*En puhu englantia. Olen kotoisin Suomesta*," calculating that it was highly unlikely I'd encounter someone from Finland in this part of the world.

As the customs man reached for my papers, I tried out a few Arabic words. I might as well have pronounced the magic formula for *Open Sesame* to gain entry to the enchanted cave. From that moment on, my life changed, all obstacles fell away, as if I had let a hundred willing genies out of the bottle. The customs man first gaped at me in astonishment, then turned to his colleagues to share the marvel. They clustered round me, completely ignoring the other passengers. How had I learned their language, where, when, and above all *why*? Why had I wanted to learn to speak their language? Hardly any foreigner ever did.

I suddenly realized that to learn a language was an act of love; you had to love someone to master his or her native tongue, whether it was your mother when you were a baby, or a girlfriend or boyfriend from another land. And these wise men from an ancient culture disdained by generations of monolingual colonialists had come to know this truth profoundly.

I was whisked through customs and the baggage area on a magic carpet of helping hands. From then on the carpet rolled out before me: finding a taxi, a hotel, a restaurant, spending a couple of days in the Lebanese mountains, then sharing a communal taxi to Syria, where I floated across the desert border on a tide of small brown boys bearing brass trays with miniature glasses of hot sweet tea, sailing me past the line-ups and visa inspections like a pasha.

Armed with little more than *Salaamu alaykum*, *Inshallah* and *Alhamdulillah* for "Peace be upon you, if God wills, God be praised," I had a verbal passport that sliced through the densest tangle of red tape. It was as if Churchill had never drawn any of his insultingly arbitrary map lines on his cognac-splattered Versailles Peace Conference stationary in Cairo in 1919, had never drawn the frontier of the newly-created Kingdom of Jordan with the strange jog in it the Arabs knew to this day as "Churchill's hiccup."

And then onto Damascus: the most beautiful city I'd ever seen that also happened to be the oldest continuously functioning human habitation on the planet, all turquoise mosaics and honeyed limestone bathed in a white light so dazzling it might have flashed about Saint Paul.

I inquired from a young man how to get to the Umayyad Mosque. Another rock instantly rolled away from the entrance to another magic cave. The university student I'd stopped not only spent the entire morning personally escorting me round the legendary mosque, but somehow managed to conjure up an instant seminar in my honor that afternoon where flocks of undergraduates pummeled my arms and shoulders as they half-jokingly quizzed me about my "imperialist ambitions" in the Middle East. (Much more about this later.)

Afterwards, they walked me back to my hotel in age-old Arab style: hand-in-hand, already not just friends but brothers.

This was turning everything upside-down, breaking all the laws of social physics, as shockingly as Einstein and Heisenberg had broken the laws of Newton. For, like an elementary particle piercing a metal plate, I could stride through customs barriers and across borders, instantly entering what in the West would be impenetrable inner circles and hermetically sealed closed shops. The rigid hierarchies of class and education and wealth that segmented life in my native land could be resolved here with an Arabic word. Their house was my house.

2

Laila would wake me at dawn with a glass of tea and a sesame seed biscuit. Every morning her deep black eyes – black as the night that was her name in Arabic – stared solemnly into mine and asked me why they were blue. She didn't know people could have blue eyes. Had I been ill?

Another recurring question was: Where was my gun? All American cowboys had guns. Six-shooters that went *bang, bang, bang, bang...* She frowned as she lost count.

Talking to a five-year old at six o'clock in the morning is a challenge at best. Talking to such a child in *Arabic* provided a dizzying view of the linguistic peaks I'd have to scale if I were ever to master a language with three times the vocabulary of English and a dozen or more different dialects.

Valiantly, I tried to explain yet again that I wasn't American or a cowboy and that where I came from hardly anybody had guns, let alone six-shooters. Laila hawked loudly and tiptoed over to the open window on her bare feet to spit outside. (The family was too poor to buy her sandals.)

The three young men I shared the small bedroom with had already left for the day. Ahmed on his unending search for a job, and his two older brothers Mahmud and Farid to the family's sole source of income, a struggling car repair business in a delapidated shack on the edge of the city. Mrs. Haidami and her elder daughter, Nour, were invisible as usual; they couldn't be seen by me when the male members of the family were absent, only Laila enjoyed that priviledge because of her young age. Nobody ever talked of what happened to Mr. Haidami.

As was soon to become my habit, I spent each morning in the Dominican library, my daily opportunity to climb back into the time machine. All I had to do was start to read any passage of written

Arabic and I'd find myself traveling down that passage through time all the way back to the Arabian desert circa 630 AD. It didn't matter whether what I was reading was from a novel or from today's headlines, it was – and always would be until the end of time – written in exactly the selfsame Arabic, letter for letter and dot for dot, that was used almost fourteen hundred centuries ago. For that was the Moment, and the only Moment, when God spoke to man.

This was the basis of Islam itself, the foundation of the faith of every Muslim: *la illaha illa Allah wa Muhammad rasul Ullah* – "There is no god but God and Muhammad is the Messenger of God." In other words – through the Angel Gabriel – God spoke to one man and one man only, out there in the sand dunes, and God dictated to that man the reading – *Al-Qur'an* (the Koran).

Because this was the one and only occasion God spoke to man since the universe began and because He chose to use the language of the desert dwellers of the day, that particular desert dialect suddenly froze as solid and immutable as the *Ka'aba* itself in Holy Mecca. If the Jews were the Chosen People, Arabic was the Chosen Language.

This fact had many ramifications. For one thing, the ancient desert dwellers hadn't yet evolved any letters for vowels. So vowel letters could never be allowed to develop, leaving all the work to the consonants. This made reading Arabic script challenging, to say the least. You had to mouth the words to read them at all, you had to sound them out.

In a sense, if you didn't already know the word or at least its context you couldn't read it. It was like trying to read a word spelled "bk", is it book or beak or bike or bake? The only solution was to throw yourself into the deep end, drown yourself in the sounds of the written words, gulp them down into your vocal chords, never quite knowing what was going to happen next – until you heard your own voice telling you. You couldn't skip ahead to see what was coming around the next sentence, you just had to plough on, one or two words at a time. So it was very difficult to be objective about what you were reading because the very act of decoding the words was so deeply involving you simply didn't have time to weigh their meaning coolly and unemotionally. That's why linguists often said Arabic script was much more "oral" and "acoustic" than any used in the West, which was only right and proper since God had *spoken* this language to Muhammad, who was illiterate.

When these spoken words did eventually get written down, they immediately took on the same divine power as speech. Which also had some interesting consequences. In Egypt, up until fairly recent times, one of the surefire ways of curing disease was to "drink the *Qur'an*" – or rather the ink in which it was written. Recipe: copy suitable verses from the Holy Book onto the inner surface of an earthenware bowl, pour in some water, stir it around until the words are completely washed off the sides of the bowl and absorbed into the water, then let the patients swallow this inky mess, drinking in the secret words, which were now transformed into sacred medicine.

The divinity of the script also meant that to this day it had to look as if it had been handwritten, for there were no printing presses in Muhammad's time and it was hard to imagine God with an IBM Selectric. This obliged even 20th century print shops to have three versions of each Arabic letter font, for the beginning, middle and end of words, so that when the fonts were strung together it looked as if the word had been written out in a flowing cursive hand.

I had first dipped my toe into this magical writing on Jasmine's postcard. Now I was up to my neck in it. Moving through a Roman script landscape back in the Western World was *Roman* in every sense of the word, with its forbidding column typefaces, with the more important text spelled out in the sternest shapes of all: the eponymous "Times Roman" of the august newspaper, its capital letters standing guard over the culture, serifs cocked at head and foot like so many epaulettes and spurs. Moving through an Arabic script landscape, on the other hand, was to saunter through an organic, lazy-lettered world where even the STOP sign – the "*qif*" – instead of standing at attention, lay flat on its back like a lizard in the sun with a fly bobbing up and down on its nose.

There were other consequences of Arabic's celestial origin. The desert dwellers all those hundreds of years ago not only lacked vowel letters, they also lacked capital letters, which fact, coupled with an absence of any kind of punctuation, made it impossible to indicate the beginning or end of what Westerners would call a "sentence." This too had hardly changed until very recent times. For God didn't divvy up His wisdom into discrete little fragments. He spouted it in one continuous stream with no beginning and no end.

The only permissible means that had been devised to indicate a new thought was to begin it with the Arabic word for "and" – *wa* – a practice the desert wanderers had absorbed from the Aramaic and Hebrew. This explained why faithful translations from the Aramaic/Hebrew-based Old Testament such as the King James Version began almost every sentence with "and", producing that unstoppable rolling thunder of continuous biblical prose:

"*And* the earth was without form *and* void *and* darkness was upon the face of the deep *and* the Spirit of God moved upon the face of the waters *and* God said let there be light *and* there was light *and* God saw the light that it was good *and* God divided the light from the darkness *and* God called the light day *and* the darkness He called light *and* the evening *and* the morning were the first day."

Now imagine the effect of that same unstoppable divine thunder rolling through even the most mundane paragraph of everyday Arabic about everything from what's on at the movies to how to make lentil soup.

As yet another echo of its divine origin, Arabic lacked a future tense, for who but God could talk about the future, which entailed by definition attempting to create what was going to happen. This accounted for the ubiquitous *Inshallah*, "If God Wills" that stood in for the English "will" or "shall" and also for the fact that traditional Arabs regarded anyone who tried to look into the future as slightly insane. So the Arabic language not only collapsed the past into the present, it ignored the future altogether, condemning all who spoke it to an endless present.

Even the Almighty's grammatical mistakes were set in stone – which caused a problem. One of my fellow students at Cambridge had devoted three years of his life to a PhD dissertation on the eccentric use of the accusative case in the *Qur'an*, a grammatical quirk that appeared to break all the rules. Islamic scholars had been struggling to explain away this anomaly for almost fourteen hundred years since it was unthinkable the Almighty could have made a mistake.

For an Arab to misuse his language, to tinker with its spelling or grammar, or worse still to try to modernize it by introducing foreign words for anything that had been invented since the 7th century was not merely blasphemous but an act of treason, a desecration of the fundamental Arab narrative. Automobiles were carts or "things that go," trains were "files of camels" and airplanes and airports were variations on the word for "bird." Shakespeare's "What's in a name? That which we call a rose by any other name would smell as sweet" made no sense at all in the Arab world where *everything* was in a name, where language was the pith and marrow of its very existence.

The Arabs had summed it all up in an adage: "Wisdom has alighted on three things: the brain of the

Franks, the hands of the Chinese and the tongue of the Arabs", and all this harking back to the eternal nature of the Holy *Qur'an.*

You didn't have to be a Muslim to believe in the sanctity of the language; it was deeply embedded in the psyche of all Arabic speakers. A number of Ahmed's friends were in fact Christian, but it didn't make a jot of difference linguistically, their speech was permeated with the same quotations taken from "The Reading" as those of the most devout Muslims.

When Ahmed returned each afternoon from yet another fruitless job search, he and his pals would escort their American cowboy to an open-air café they called the *muntazah* (recreation ground) where the President of Egypt, Gamal Abdul Nasser, exhorted us through loud speakers to drive Israel into the sea. If it had been in any other language, we might have had a chance to analyze the message, to criticize it. But in Arabic, whether you were Palestinian, Egyptian, Lebanese, Syrian, Muslim or Christian, it was irresistible stuff by definition uncriticizable. For every word and phrase Nasser uttered was in the language of the *Qur'an*, the voice of God ringing down the centuries.

So it was impossible to understand what was really going on when an Arab leader addressed his people if you didn't know the language. No translation could come close. It wasn't like going from German to English or even from Hindu to English. It was more like going from another galaxy to our own. In every sense of the word, Arabic was a different script that told a different story. And all because of that moment almost fourteen hundred years ago that had deified both its spoken and written form.

I had been brought up on the joke confirmed by generations of movies that God was an Englishman who spoke with an upper-class accent delivered by a classically trained actor such as Laurence Olivier. Now I knew that God's language was in fact Arabic. All these years, Olivier had been miscast, it should been Omar Sharif, or better still, Gamal Abdel Nasser who was yet again exhorting us to drown the Israelis in the Mediterranean.

"So what are we waiting for? Into the sea, into the sea!" all the young men would chant in the *muntazah*, as I to my own astonishment joined in.

3

Ahmed held up a cabbage. "This is a miracle, Abu Bassam" he said, for that was my new Arab name, the "Father of the Smiling One", because that was what my new friends had noticed I was always doing.

"Imagine," continued Ahmed, "that you had bought it on the other side of the wall, in the Israeli-occupied half of Jerusalem. Would you like to know how much that cabbage cost to produce?"

I had no idea. Ahmed told me in Jordanian dinars, and pointed out that this was about ten times what you could sell the cabbage for.

My friends crowded in on me to tell me why: notably, Ibrahim, a gentle bull of a young man, with bulging muscles and an incongruously ginger brush cut, who liked to give me bone-shattering punches on the arm, and Abd al-Haqq ("the Slave of Truth"), a tall, thin, handsome intellectual who spoke perfect English after post-graduate work in England in "various places", plus several others whose names I could never remember, in addition of course to my genial host, Ahmed.

I learned that this cabbage explained everything about the two different planets that existed side by side in their beautiful city, held apart by a United Nations' partition. To clinch their arguments, my friends took me along a narrow winding lane in the Old City, then up some almost comically crooked steps onto a rooftop.

When I looked down at my immediate surroundings, I saw the now familiar labyrinths of tiny hole-in-the-wall shops with their cobblers and brass beaters and weavers, the labyrinthine lanes thronged with a cross-section of humanity cutting through time and space.

Twentieth-century tourists rubbed shoulders with medieval monks from Greece, Armenia and Egypt; gnarled old men in traditional *kuffiyahs* and long robes played backgammon in pokey little cafes; dwarves out of the Arabian Nights staggered under mountains of battered furniture piled six feet in the air on their backs; bare-foot children played in the dust with goats and chickens.

Then my friends turned me to look down over the Old City wall into West Jerusalem, and I saw... Miami Beach: corporate franchises and neon lights, snappy logos and gaudy billboards, pizza parlors and hotdog stands, teeming with people dressed almost exclusively in modern attire.

When had their space ship landed? What universe did these aliens come from?

From Russia and Poland, from Golders Green and the Bronx, explained my friends. These white-skinned immigrants who claimed they used to live here some two thousand years ago and now sought redress for generations of persecution by finally returning home to an "uninhabited desert", which they had then turned back into what they imagined was their ancestral land of milk and honey as described in their religious books.

"And have they really turned the desert green?" I asked.

"In some areas, yes," admitted the Slave of Truth, "hence the cabbage. Billions of American dollars can indeed work miracles. There is no limit to how much water you can pour on the sand, how much agriculture you can subsidize. They're not called 'greenbacks' for nothing. Who cares if you can only sell your cabbage for a tenth of its cost?"

That evening, as the *muntazah* chanted the usual Nasser-inspired refrain, my voice grew stronger. "So what are we waiting for?" I cried, along with the others. "Into the sea, into the sea..."

4

I wondered if I could ever plumb the depths of my friends' bitterness, their moral outrage at the godawful injustice of their situation. Could I ever really imagine what it must be like, day after day, month after month, year after year, to see an alien occupation of over fourth-fifths of the land you and your ancestors have lived on for – how long was it? – almost fourteen hundred years*, just about as long as the very words on your lips and in your books and your newspapers have been Holy? For shortly after Muhammad received *The Reading* from God, he was moved to launch his astonishing Arab conquest of half the known world, including the land of Palestine, and from that day until almost the end of the 19th century, according to reams of statistics – compiled by Israeli historian no less – the population of this Palestinian land had been overwhelmingly Arab. *(*Note that there had, of course, also been Palestinians in Palestine dating back at least to Roman times. Herod the Great, the Roman-appointed King of Judaea – 37 B.C. to 4 B.C. – was himself a Palestinian Arab, having been born and bred in the place, as had many of his subjects. Note also that by 1850 the population of Palestine consisted of approximately 475,000 Palestinians and 25,000 Jews. For centuries these groups had lived in a balanced harmony: approximately 95% Palestinian and 5% Jewish.)*

Then the Zionist movement was born and Jews from the aforementioned Russia and Poland and Golders Green and the Bronx and God knows where else started to "return." Perhaps their ancestors had once lived in this place up until around 70 A.D. when the Romans kicked almost of them out, perhaps not. Did I know where my ancestors were nineteen hundred years ago? But in any event, this return and subsequent takeover of 78% of Palestine in 1948 made about as much sense as the Welsh coming down from their mountains to take over 78% of the England their ancient Celtic ancestors had once dominated.

"You really don't like Jews, do you?" I said.

My friends looked at me as if I were crazy. In biblical terms, they explained, the Arabs and the Jews were brothers, for they had the same forebear, Abraham, whose two sons, Ishmael and Isaac, were the ancestors of their two nations, Ishmael of the Arabs, and Isaac of the Jews. In everyday modern terms, they were also brothers: when my friends were little children before the founding of the State of Israel, they had grown up with Jews, many of their closest playmates had been Jews. But these were Jews from *here*, they looked like us, you couldn't tell us apart. They were *Sabra* (from the Hebrew *sabrah*, literally "prickly pear"), Jews born in Palestine, Jews who did actually belong here, who were named after the thorny fruit of the cactus grown on this tough, arid earth. Whereas the pallid softies who had now overrun their land were mainly *Ashkenazim* (from the Hebrew *Ashkĕnāz*, the medieval rabbinical name for Germany), they were western colonizers, just another occupying power in the long line of imperialists who had gobbled up so many Arab lands.

"So you aren't anti-Semitic?" I asked.

More astonished looks.

"How can we be anti-Semitic," said Ibrahim, "we *are* Semitic, for – again in Biblical terms – in addition to being the co-descendants of Abraham, the Arabs and the Jews were also the sons of Shem. Let me remind you: Noah had three sons, Japeth, Ham and Shem. Japeth begat the Indo-Europeans, Ham begat the Hamitic peoples – the Berbers of North Africa – and Shem begat the Semitic peoples, the Arabs and the Jews. Even my own name," noted Ibrahim, "is simply the Arabic form of 'Abraham'."

"Strictly speaking," said the Slave of Truth, "the word 'Semitic' is a linguistic term – like 'Indo-European' – applying to a family of languages that included Hebrew, Arabic and Aramaic."

"So *you're* Semitic, Abu Bassam, since you speak Arabic!" cried Ibrahim. "*Yallah, Abu Bassam, alhamdullilah!*" He gave me another of his hefty punches.

It was like listening to a library of walking encyclopedias reeling off fact after fact. Back home, my friends and I talked about girls and pints of bitter and rock and roll, but never of politics, about which we knew next to nothing. But here, my new Arab chums talked about almost nothing *but* politics in their daily gatherings in the *muntazah*.

Should there ever be a temporary lull in our political discourse, the ever-present booming voice of Nasser, our latter-day Saladin, would soon get us back on track. How we loved this man, how his melodious Koranic phrases, coming straight from the divine horse's mouth, resonated in our hearts. How we chanted his name *Nasser Nasser Nasser Habibina Habibina Habibina*: "Our Darling One."

But where were the darling ones we should have

been obsessing about? I asked them, looking round the exclusively male occupants of the *muntazah*. Where were our Jasmines?

"We'll show you on Sunday afternoon," said Ibrahim. And they all laughed.

5

"Ma bidi minak illa bayyin sinnak", as the most famous Lebanese *chanteuse* of all time liked to sing: "All I want from you is the baring of your teeth," the equivalent of *My Mammy's,* "I'd walk a thousand miles for one of your smiles."

We didn't have to walk quite that far, but it was still a bit of a hike to the only place in my friends' part of Arab Jerusalem where you could make eye contact with a girl: the lobby of the local cinema on a Sunday afternoon (a holiday for both Muslims and Christians), since this was the only showing of the week that permitted a mixed audience for its Egyptian comedies and melodramas starring the great comic Ismail Yassine and the dramatic actor Hussain Riyadh.

There they were, dozens of visions of unveiled loveliness, with lavish applications of kohl around the eyes and shimmering cascades of hair, emerged from their cocoon for this brief butterfly moment. Each girl was accompanied by a chaperone, usually her mother, warned Ahmed, making sure we didn't get too close, let alone actually talk to any of them. But we could exchange glances.

So we chatted together across the lobby with our

eyes. "What happens if one of the pairs of eyes says yes?" I asked my brothers, "Could you pass her a note or something?"

"You could write a note," replied Ahmed, "but you couldn't give it to her directly. "You'd have to have some older female in your family give it to the girl's chaperone, and then, if you were very lucky, she might permit you to talk to the girl – but only in the chaperone's presence of course."

"So what do you do when you – you know – "

They stopped me before I could go any further. They didn't even want to talk about it. Suddenly, my brothers who had been so open about everything else, letting me enter their innermost circle and sharing their most intimate thoughts, had lowered a taboo curtain, hiding the sexual part of their lives from view, veiling it as completely as their women.

This taboo explained why, although I shared a bedroom with three other young men, I never saw any of them in their underwear, let alone naked, as would have been perfectly normal in the West. It was also perhaps related to the *faux pas* I made another Saturday when I was going to join Mahmud at his garage to drive down to Jericho to bathe in the Dead Sea. I'd rolled up my bathing suit in a towel and started out of the house – only to be pulled back by Ahmed, who whispered that it wasn't proper to carry an exposed towel in public, you had to wrap it in paper.

Of course Abd al-Haqq had an explanation for this towel business the next time I got him alone. It was because a towel may have touched a bare body: guilt by association, an accessory to the crime, so to speak. But this hypersensitivity to the body wasn't just about sex, it went much deeper than that. Why did I think Islamic carpets displayed such elaborate geometrical designs, all those rosettes and lozenges and stylized flower and calligraphic motifs? Why all that abstraction? Because Islam forbade the representation of any animate being, human or animal. Just as having a future tense in your language would be playing God by creating the future, so depicting a living being in your visual art would be playing God by creating life. On top of that, however much the patterns of rosettes and lozenges spiraled all over the place, they always returned to where they started, for it was also forbidden to preempt God by ever creating something that had a beginning or an end.

So Islam not only concealed your beach towel in brown paper, it tied your social life into knots as tight as its rugs.

6

"Ten paces is about right," said Ahmed, "as long as you don't get any closer than that, we'll be fine."

I was enjoying a rare privilege, a shopping expedition with the women of the family. By now, I had already met Mrs. Haidami and her older daughter Noor within the confines of the house, but only one bit at a time: first their hands as they passed food through the kitchen door to the males of the family, then as they gradually let their guard down, their arms, and their faces, and eventually all of them. Even this was only permissible when one of the males in the family was present and provided they were all safely concealed inside the house. But to go out in public with the women was quite another thing. The only way to accomplish this was for the women to walk at least ten paces behind us.

I badgered Ahmed with questions, "Why this seclusion of women? Why – with the exception of the butterfly moment in the cinema lobby on Sunday afternoons – did they have to cover every strand of their hair and every inch of their arms and legs when out in public?"

For some time Ahmed was reluctant to talk about this at all, but he eventually broke down. It's in the *Qur'an*, he explained, and recited the verse that says women must not reveal their charms to any adult male outside their immediate family.

When I pressed him for a more in-depth explanation, Ahmed just shrugged and said, "It is written."

It was time for another session with the Slave of Truth. "Look," said Abd al-Haqq, "a woman's body and her hair, what the *Qur'an* calls her 'adornments' attract men, do they not?"

I had to admit that this was so.

"Would you try to imagine that you had a wife?"

I agreed to try.

Now it was my turn to face a barrage of questions. "Why on earth would you want your wife to attract other men? Wouldn't that risk breaking up the family?

What is the divorce rate in the West?"

"I don't know," I replied, "somewhere between forty and fifty percent."

"So what exactly is the point of having married women going around trying to seduce other men with their charms? Unmarried women could do this provided their behavior was strictly controlled as in the Sunday cinema ritual, but why on earth would you want your wife to do it?"

"Freedom," I suggested. "Women should be free to do what they want, just like men."

"But they are free here," said Abd a-Haqq, "precisely because they *are* decently covered they are free to walk the streets without being ogled or cat-called or harassed, and they are also free to become doctors or lawyers or university professors just as in the West, even television and radio presenters. Which was the first radio station in the world to have a female announcer?"

"The BBC," I ventured.

"No, it was Kuwait radio many years before either Britain or America."

"Okay," I admitted, "but I was talking about women having the same freedom as men to wear what they like and be as attractive as the like. Surely that choice should be left up to the women themselves?"

"Family, family, family," riposted Abd al-Haqq, "that's the whole basis of our society, the rock on which it is built. If that rock starts to crack, everything falls apart. Have you ever compared the crime rates in the West with those in the Middle East? And don't say ours are low because we cut people's hands off, because we don't, that's only done – and very rarely – in the most extremist Islamic countries such as Saudi Arabia, which follows the the religious law, the *Shari'a*, to the letter. In Palestine, our law is exactly the same as in Europe."

"Is the crime rate in Palestine, really that low?"

"There's a bench on the pavement of the busy street in front of the Haidami house," said Abd al-Haqq. "If you leave twenty dinars on that bench tomorrow morning, I'll bet you anything that it will still be there when you come back in the evening."

The following morning, I did as he suggested. When I came home some eight hours later, my money hadn't moved.

"So you see," said Abd al-Haqq that evening, "freedom means different things to different people. Our Arab family values give our women freedom from sexual harassment – not to mention an almost zero divorce rate – and our Islamic values give all of us freedom from crime, just as the Islamic requirement to donate 10% of our wealth to the poor gives us freedom from want. In the West, you have none of these freedoms. Instead you are free to be mugged and beaten and left to die of poverty and sickness while your women are harassed and humiliated and quite often raped. In return, your women are free to walk around half-naked. Some trade off."

7

The men held the palms of their hands together in a cross between a prayer and a Brahmin salutation and then suddenly shot to the other end of the moral spectrum with a copulatory jerking up and down of their joined hands as they snapped their forefingers together with an ear-splitting report like the crack of a whip. The faster they cracked the whip, the faster the muscles of the dancer's bare stomach gyrated, breaking in wave after fleshy wave on the gold-trimmed skirt slung low over her hips as her arms undulated like Edenic snakes trailing a succession of semi-transparent veils across her face and body, all the time shaking her almost naked breasts in our faces.

The orchestra's instruments were a madman's distorted visions of drums and guitars and harps, musical swamp monsters dreamed up by some Oriental Francis Bacon – until I realized they were the primordial versions of the familiar modern Western instruments that had somehow got stuck in time. The music itself seemed equally twisted out of shape, slow when I expected fast, fast when I expected slow, and endlessly, hypnotically, wailingly repetitive, until it reached what I assumed was the end of an octave only to break through this barrier and continue on into a no-man's land of fractional notes uncharted by any melody I had ever heard.

Although these sounds were new to me, I felt instinctively they were as archaic as the instruments. Had God also frozen music in time fourteen hundred years ago? If, as Goethe said, architecture was frozen music, then I was listening to one heck of an old building. Even the dancer's voluptuous movements seemed primeval, as if part of the ancient landscape. This was surely pre-Islamic body language, from Herod's time at least I could have sworn, and Salome was still at it, still able to have our heads on a platter at the drop of just one last libidinous fragment of gauze.

During a pause in the performance – which was taking place in that "den of iniquity" as some of the stricter Palestinians called the town of Ramallah, a few miles north of Jerusalem – I remarked to Abd al-Haqq how weird Arabic music sounded compared to regular, mainstream music.

He laughed, "Your ethnocentrism is showing again, Abu Bassam. Our music is the mainstream, your Western music is the oddball tributary."

He explained that what we'd been listening to was based on by far the most widely used musical scale in the world, the pentatonic five-note scale developed throughout Asia by virtually all preliterate cultures. Arabic music had at least twenty different versions of this scale called *Maqams,* many of which used quarter flats and sharps. Western classical music in contrast, only had one scale, the diatonic or heptatonic (seven-note) scale, which in global terms was the odd man out.

Once again, I was reminded that my Arab friends quite literally marched to a different drummer

After Salome had executed her final belly roll and shimmied off the dance floor amidst a flurry of finger cymbals, I asked my friend if he didn't see a contradiction between the Arab obsession with hiding women's charms from the male gaze, and what we'd all just witnessed.

He had me here too, "That's the whole point, don't you see? It makes it all the more fun, all the more erotic."

"But isn't this hypocrisy, a double-standard, like Victorian England, one rule for the woman and another for the man?"

"When the man spent all night in a brothel and then went back to a home where even the piano legs were covered and a wife who'd learned to 'lie back and think of England.'"

"Right."

"Wrong. It isn't a bit like Victorian England. That's what you Westerners never seem to get. We *like* these contradictions. You wallow in Viennese guilt about them, we revel in them. You bury them in your subconscious and have to go to shrinks to dig them up. As James Joyce put it, 'You are Jung and easily Freudened.' Here we are much older than you in every sense of the word and the situation couldn't be more different. You've seen what goes on in the *souq*, haven't you?"

I had in fact, thanks to Ahmed and the others, been able to make quite a study of the Arabic open-air market place known as the *souq*.

My friends would sit me down in one of the tiny shops in the Old City, wait for the little boy to bring the inevitable glass of tea, and then we would just watch. It was pure theater. In comes a customer to inquire the price of a carpet. The merchant sends for the little boy again (it was amazing how many little boys here never seemed to go to school). Seller and buyer then sit sipping their tea and enjoying a puff or two of tobacco inhaled through rose water via a hubble-bubble pipe, aka *shisha*, *nargile* or *hookah*. After a short while, the merchant wipes away a tear and embarks on a litany of personal tragedies, from imminent bankruptcy to dying parents, starving children and assorted incurable diseases, all obliging him to give away this extraordinary, magnificent heirloom of a Shiraz carpet at such a derisory price he's embarrassed even to say it out loud. The customer urges him to overcome his embarrassment. The merchant eventually gives in and names his price, 1300 dinars. The customer leaps to his feet, trembling with anger, and storms out of the shop, declaring that he's never been so insulted in all his life and will never set foot on the premises again, let God be his witness.

With such precise timing you'd swear they'd rehearsed the scene a thousand times, the merchant waits until the very last split-second before darting after the customer and pulling him back inside the shop. This will be the death of his business and very probably the death of himself and everyone in his family, not to mention the everlasting shame of his ancestors, but he is willing to reduce the price to 1,200 dinars. 600 parries the customer, suddenly not in the least angry. 1100 cries the shopkeeper. And off they go, darting and weaving, cut and thrust: 650 vs. 1,050, 700 vs. 1,000, 750 vs. 950, 800 vs. 900, 825 vs. 875, with the duel finally resulting in a draw at 850 dinars without a drop of blood being spilled. They shake hands and sit down again, the very best of friends over their tea and pipe.

Finally, the customer saunters out of the shop with his carpet, and the merchant claps his hands in delight.

Feeling oh so worldly-wise, I turned to my friends to say of course it wasn't worth half that.

"Terribly sorry," said Abd al-Haqq ruefully, but actually it was worth at least 1000 dinars. The point of haggling isn't to get the best price, it's to get the best haggle, it's for the love of the sport. The merchants of the *souq* would rather lose money than lose the fun of bargaining. When a European or American barges in and pays the asking price right off the bat, they're depressed for the rest of the day." He sighed, "Sometimes I think you people are living in an irony free zone."

I was beginning to understand: life in the Middle East was a kaleidoscope of paradoxes. I'd been profoundly shocked when I first saw a man beat his donkey or another man kick his dog for no reason, or when I'd heard small boys boast of how many sparrows they'd slaughtered before breakfast with their slingshots. How could they hate animals so? How could their attitudes towards creatures that would be beloved pets in the West be so different?

Once again, Abd al-Haqq had put me straight, "It wasn't that they didn't like animals, just that the animals they liked were not the same ones Westerners liked. In England, people loved their dogs and cats but tortured foxes, in Spain they tormented bulls, in

Germany they massacred young deer, in France they feasted on horse meat."

"So what animals do the Arabs like?" I asked.

"The horse and the camel, but above all, the camel", said the Slave of Truth. "*Ibn kalb*, 'son of a dog', was one of the worst Arab insults, but to be likened to a camel was one of the highest compliments. Which made sense. After all, every Arab descended ultimately from the desert where the camel made the difference between life and death, providing transport, food, fuel, clothing and shelter. The *Qur'an* said, 'The Almighty in making animals created nothing preferable to the camel.' It was no accident that the Arabic word for camel was *jamal* and the Arabic word for beauty was *jamaal*."

I was a long way from a world where a camel was a horse designed by a committee.

"Look at this," summed up Abd al-Haqq, raising yet another glass of what I had at first thought was milk, only to learn from my omniscient friend that it was *arak*, the world's oldest liqueur, made from aniseed berries mixed with distilled palm wine and first concocted in Egypt around 800 B.C. The Greeks subsequently copied it as *ouzo*, the Turks as *raki*, (also known as 'lion's milk') and the French as *anise* or *pastis* or *Pernod* or *Ricard* (the latter because it was produced by the firm of that name); the drink had almost as many names as God.

He went on to explain that when first poured out of the bottle, *arak* was an inoffensive looking colorless liquid that turned a virginal white when you added water as if to disguise the fact that it had a kick like a mule. Yet another irony that went clean over Western heads, for we'd always assumed the Islamic ban on drinking alcohol meant that Muslims didn't drink. But like the belly dancer, it was all the sexier because it was absolutely forbidden and never happened. A huge joke all round.

How apt that the language God used to dictate the Holy Book, which banned alcohol, should also be the language that gave us the word in the first place, *al-kuhul*, from the verb meaning to distill something whether it be a drink or the black powder – the *kohl* – that both the Sunday afternoon girls and the belly dancers smeared so liberally on their eyelids.

Speaking of which, here she comes again.

I downed my umpteenth glass of *arak*, really "milking the lion" now, as I put my hands together in prayer in order to snap my forefingers.

8

"How's the 'School for Spies'?" That was one of the running jokes whenever I took my usual place in the *muntazah* each afternoon.

Patiently, I would explain yet again that before coming to Jerusalem the place I'd visited for a few days in the tiny village of Shemlan in the mountains above Beirut was the *Middle East Center for Arab Studies*. It was simply a language school where people in the British armed forces could take crash courses in colloquial Arabic. It had nothing to do with spying. Nothing whatever. I'd just gone there to take one of its crash courses myself.

"So you are working for the British government?" said my friends.

"No, I'm not. They let ordinary students in as well sometimes. I was recommended by a friend in the Royal Air Force I met at Cambridge."

I thought back to the dozen or so army and air force officers who had suddenly turned up in my beginning Arabic language classes. Two in particular from the RAF had become close friends.

"Squadron-Leader Jeffrey ffoulkes-Willoughby, two small f's," one of them had announced when we were first introduced. Handlebar mustache, leather jacket, MG, he was straight out of a *Carry On* movie. In the middle of a perfectly amicable conversation he would suddenly pretend to be insulted, start to take off his jacket and ask you, "Do you want to come outside, dear boy?"

Flight-Lieutenant Richard Wycliffe-Foster, on the other hand, was soft-spoken and immensely intelligent, with a weakness for medieval brass rubbings, Gregorian chants and apparently indispensable Latin locutions such as *heterobalneopote*, an inveterate drinker of other people's bath water. He was a pretty good linguist too, putting poor old ffoulkes-Willoughby for shame for obviously not having the slightest talent for learning any language, let alone one as demanding as Arabic. However, it had been two small f's who had given me an introduction to the Shemlan language school. It wasn't until much later that I was to understand why.

Meanwhile, my Palestinian brothers would continue their teasing: if I wasn't a spy, then I had to admit that I was at least an agent for *al-Isti'mar* – Imperialism – which must have been the most frequently used word in their vocabulary.

Was this payback for thirty years of humiliation under the British Mandate? Again, it was the Slave of Truth who set me straight. "As a matter of fact," he explained, "the mandate was probably the happiest period in recent Palestinian history: the trains and buses ran on time (where had I heard *that* before), the post arrived on time, the telephones worked – they'd even had red pillar boxes and telephone boxes – and people stood in line to queue up for things."

I smiled. All that was left now of British queuing theory was the Palestinian version of a rugger scrum. First of all, forget anything about designated bus stops; they were for beginners. Every experienced Palestinian bus rider knew that you stopped a bus when you needed to get on, regardless of where it was going or how fast it was traveling.

Once stopped, the next objective was for everyone to charge at the bus door simultaneously in a glorious head-on collision. Having fought your way inside, it was now your duty to fight for a seat as fiercely as possible. Having secured that, order suddenly prevailed and everyone immediately became the best of friends again. Should an elderly man or a veiled woman board the bus, the driver would yell at one of the young men to surrender his seat, which he would do without a murmur.

Going to the cinema was another indicator of how thoroughly the Palestinians had shucked off their British training. After the usual fight to the death to get inside the place, their behavior gave a whole new meaning to the term "active participation", with non-stop talking back at the screen and clambering over seats and shoulders.

They were like a bunch of newly-weds who couldn't keep their hands off each other. They not only held each other's hands and kissed each other repeatedly on each cheek, they also rejoiced in pummeling one another as frequently as possible; an unending teddy bears' picnic.

The biggest pummeler of all was Ibrahim – as my arms bore witness. But of course, as the Slave of Truth kept telling me, it was merely yet another paradox: the more Ibrahim bashed you about, the more he loved you.

9

Ibrahim's heart really was as big as his biceps. Whenever he could scrape together the money, he'd buy food to take to a small village just outside Bethlehem where some of his relatives lived.

He'd invited me to go with him once. I had never seen or smelled such poverty in my life. The Haidamis were hard up, God knows, but Ibrahim's aunt and uncle and their nine children might have stepped out of a Dickensian poor house. Scrawny chickens scrabbled across the dirt floor of their one-room shack built from rusty oil drums and old tyres as brown streams of raw sewage oozed along the gutter outside their front door. Worst of all were with the flies and the children: the obscene polarity of the perfect little angel faces dozing in the suffocating heat contrasting with the black shit-engorged creatures crawling across their eyelids and inside their open mouths.

What was this place? The First Circle of Hell?

Ibrahim was surprised I didn't know. It was one of scores of Palestinian refugee camps 750,000 Palestinians had been forced to flee to after 1948, *al-Nakba*, the catastrophe, as the Arabs called it, the process of forcing Palestinians out of their homes and into exile after the United Nations partitioned Palestine.

Unemployment in the camps was nearly total, many of the men being without work for as long as they could remember. The only thing that saved these desperate, despairing people from complete starvation were the bare-bones food subsidies of UNWRA and the contributions of bravehearts such as Ibrahim, who were only marginally better off themselves.

At the Haidami's, I was never allowed to pay for a single thing. Surely, now was my chance? My university scholarship made me a millionaire compared with these poor souls. Amazingly, even here there was a tea boy. I reached into my pocket – and was immediately stopped by Ibrahim's uncle. I was their guest. But couldn't I at least offers them some cigarettes – even if they were the Jordanian kind you had to hold whole horizontally to stop the tobacco falling out?

Ahlan wa sahlan, said the uncle. Didn't I know what that meant? I was their guest. Their house was my house, their possessions were my possessions. Didn't I know that?

I had been humbled yet again. Yes, I knew, I also knew that I would never forget these people. The poorer they were, the more they wanted to give you. I'd once made the mistake of admiring a picture in the Haidami house. Ahmed had immediately taken it off the wall and handed it to me. "It is yours." I felt almost relieved there was nothing on the walls of the refugee camp to admire.

As Ibrahim I rode back on the bus to Jerusalem, I couldn't stop talking about his relatives' extraordinary hospitality. Ibrahim responded with a story:

> *Once upon a time there was a very poor man with the name of Hatem whose only possession in the world was a beautiful Arabian horse, the swiftest animal in the desert. One day a sumptuously dressed stranger stopped by Hatem's threadbare tent. As was the custom, before asking the stranger his business, Hatem insisted that he take his rest while he prepared him a meal. After the stranger had enjoyed the meal, which was truly delicous, Hatem asked him the purpose of his visit. The man answered that the*

King had heard about Hatem's wonderful horse and had sent him to offer a large sack of gold for it. Hatem suddenly cried out in great sorrow. What is the matter, said the visitor, just bring me the horse and you will be a rich man. I cannot, replied Hatem, you have just eaten it.

It was the time machine again. The place where I'd just been entertained so generously may have looked like a twentieth-century refugee camp, but it was in fact simply the latest metamorphosis of Hatem's tent. Right next door to Bethlehem of all places. How appropriate. The place where – at least for Christians – the greatest goodness the world had ever known was born. Jesus' parents were outcasts, refugees, with nowhere to live. If UNWRA had been around at the time they would put the son of God in a camp.

In the *muntazah*, the discussion of *al-Isti'mar* rambled on. If it wasn't the British Mandate they were continually going on about, I remarked, exactly what imperalism were they referring to? As if I didn't know.

It was Israel of course, always Israel, a gaping wound in their sides, a running sore infecting every aspect of their lives like the river of sewage in the camp. To the Palestinians, the establishment of Israel was nothing more nor less than naked imperialism, a western colony dumped down on their land to stick out like a sore thumb in the midst of their ancestral orange orchards and olive groves and fourteen-hundred-year-old Holy sites.

The Israelis did this, the Israelis did that. The very way they pronounced the word in Arabic sounded like the hiss of a snake in their lost Garden of Eden. Whenever one of them said the hated world, Laila-like, he would hawk loudly and turn away to spit. I wondered if in pre-Israel days people used to spit so much, and if so, was it simply to clear their throats of the sand blowing in from the desert?

Abd al-Haqq told me that a group of them were getting involved with some Egyptian friends in the planning of a rebel organization for the liberation of Palestine. One suggested title was *Munazzama at-tahrir al-filasastinya* – the Palestine Liberation Organization. Sounded pretty good, didn't it? Would I like to join?

10

"Arabic poetry is like a string of pearls," said Abd al-Haqq, his nose in a book as usual. "Western poetry nearly always had a story line, a beginning, a middle and an end. That had been true ever since Aristotle laid out his theory of the three-act structure of drama in his *Poetics*. Arab poets didn't think like that. Each segment of a poem was a pearl, complete and perfect in itself. These pearls were then strung together in a sequence, any sequence, it didn't matter, the order was of no importance. Not only that, but the string of pearls formed a circle round your neck, a literary necklace of perpetual beauty, endlessly recursive, with no beginning and no end, just like those oriental carpets.

I looked around the *muntazah*, where so many of the men were never without their string of prayer beads, turning and turning in their hands. Like their deep sense of irony, were these eternal circles the real essence of the Arab soul?

"They certainly run very deep and far," said Abd al-Haqq, "thousands of years in fact, all the way back to pre-Islamic Bedouin poetry."

"Oh yes, the *Bedu*," laughed Ibrahim, breaking the mood, as Charlie Chaplin-like he mimed watching a fly settle on his cheek, then slapped his face and pretended to eat the squashed insect.

They all exploded into laughter, this was one of their favorite jokes, given all the more punch by their belief that flies were made of excrement since that's all they seemed to live on, courtesy of the less than perfect sanitary arrangements in so many parts of the Middle East. For the Palestinians, the unsavory flies symbolized the love-hate relationship they had with the Bedouin, who were all Jordanians as far as they were concerned.

What was wrong with the Jordanians?

Again, the Slave of Truth had the explanation: after the Israelis – as compensation for nineteen hundred years of persecution at the hands of just about everyone *except* the Arabs – had exacted their pound of flesh in the form of 78% of Palestine, the UN placed most of what was left over – the infamous Left Bank – in the care of the Kingdom of Jordan.

The Palestinians deeply resented being made subservient to Jordan, whose people they thought of as

Bedu, primitive sheep-herding desert nomads lording it over their own urbane and sophisticated culture. In particular, they bristled at the arrogant flying visits the young King Hussein would pay to his Palestinian people in Jerusalem, careering down their narrow streets at breakneck speed in heavily-armed convoys of gigantic Cadillacs as machine-gun toting soldiers lined the street on either side and motorcycle outriders drove straight at the crowd to force them to make way. On top of all this, you were obliged to applaud as the great King flew by. Or else.

I was surprised at how cynical my friends were about this monarch, who was such a hero in the West. They explained to me that he was just another spoilt, corrupt tyrant in the pay of the American and British imperialists, living in no fewer than three gigantic palaces in jarring contrast with their beloved Nasser, a fervent socialist who practiced what he preached by living in a modest house just like everyone else. (Their dislike of Hussein wasn't entirely misplaced: a few years later he was to massacre five thousand Palestinian refugees in Jordan.)

But my brothers disdain for the Bedouin was an even greater shock for me at the time, for I'd been brought up on desert adventure stories in which noble Bedouins partnered with equally noble Brits such as Sir Wilfred Thesiger, the first man to cross the Empty Quarter of the Arabian Desert; St. John Philby, another desert explorer and adviser to King Saud; the great Lawrence of Arabia of course; and Glubb Pasha, the fabled British commander of the Jordanian Arab

Legion.

My friends hadn't heard of Thesiger or Philby and considered Lawrence to have been a traitor to the Arabs ("A drum, all noise with a hollow inside his head.") But Glubb, now he was a real hero, even if he had worked for Jordan. They never tired of relating how Glubb Pasha spoke such fluent Bedouin Arabic that he would play tricks on his own men by dressing up as a flea-bitten *Bedu* crouching in the dusty gutter and holding out his hands as he begged for alms for the love of God. If the soldier he was importuning failed to pay up, he'd leap to his feet and give the poor sod the fright of his life.

As we strolled home from the *muntazah* munching on the *falafel* (a fried pattie of hummus, onion, garlic and sesame oil) we always bought from street vendors after an afternoon of politics, the Palestinian equivalent of the chicken curry that rounded out a pub night back in England, I wondered just what it was that attracted so many of my countrymen to the Arabian desert. What did they all have in common?

"An astonishing amount, as a matter of fact," said Abd al-Haqq as he pulled on my hand to hold me back behind the others, "they all spoke fluent Arabic, they all went to Oxford or Cambridge and most of them were spies who liked men."

I dropped his hand as if it were a burning coal. "I'm not like that!"

He laughed: "You're not a spy or you don't like men? I know you go to Cambridge and you certainly speak Arabic."

I looked down at his hand.

"Another irony for you, Abu Bassam. Holding hands is a sign of masculinity for us, just like growing a mustache."

He took my hand again. "I don't mean you like men, or that you're a spy, in spite of how much we tease you, but the others on the list – well, learning Arabic and spying and Oxbridge and homosexuality do seem to go together." He started to count off on his fingers: "Lawrence, an Arabist, went to Oxford, undoubtedly a spy, and there's strong evidence he was at least bisexual; Thesiger, also an Oxford Arabist, don't know if he was a spy, but he was a misogynist who admitted his love of boys and – "

" – St. John Philby," I chimed in, "Cambridge Arabist probably a spy but certainly the father of the double agent Kim Philby: Arabic, Cambridge – not sure he was gay, but given his friendship with Burgess and McLean – "

"...both of whom went to King's College, Cambridge – have you seen those choirboys? – both dabbled in Arabic, both became double agents, and both – well, we know for sure that Burgess was homosexual and McLean partly so, so they were nearly all – "

"Queens of England," I muttered.

"What?"

"Oh, nothing." I was thinking of Wycliffe-Foster. Could he be a spy? He certainly met all the other criteria.

"Sometimes I think you're almost as secretive as we

are," laughed Abd al-Haqq. "Maybe that's the key to all this: after all, what do these factors – spying and homosexuality, and Arabic and Oxbridge – have in common? They're all related to secretiveness, to hiding your true self from the world. We Arabs are past masters at this, but foreigners – and particularly certain types of Englishmen – can also use our opaque language and culture as a cloak to hide behind, a 'cover' as they say in the trade."

"And by 'certain types'", I added, "you're referring to people from privileged backgrounds who went to private boarding schools and to Oxbridge where you're trained never to reveal what you're really thinking?"

"Exactly. Now add in homosexuality – which the private schools don't exactly discourage – and you compound the secrecy. Homosexuals are used to living double lives, to clandestine meetings in darkened public lavatories on Hampstead Heath, they're split personalities by nature, perfect candidates to become double agents. Closets within closets."

"By the way, Abd al-Haqq," I broke in, "you said you studied in various places in England. Where exactly?"

He smiled, "Kings College, Cambridge. Where else?"

11

Privacy. The word apparently didn't exist in Arabic. There was certainly no shortage of words for secrecy and hiding, but nothing to describe the state of being withdrawn from the society of others. Twenty-four hours a day, I was with other people: sharing a bedroom with three other young men, then the house full of the coming and going of yet more people, the streets where other young men flocked to my side, the tiny shops that were always abuzz with other people's conversations, the *muntazah* where I never once saw anyone sitting alone.

Sartre said *l'Enfer c'est les Autres*. Maybe that was going a bit far, but one thing I knew, in the Middle East you couldn't even escape to the lavatory. Well, you could, but people sitting only a couple of feet away would continue to talk to you over and under the flimsy excuse for a door, which had huge gaps at top and bottom. Even that was a semi-communal experience.

And yet – always with the exception of Abd al-Haqq –they were all just as prudish when it came to talking about elimination as they were about discussing sex. I only ever heard one reference to bodily functions, and that was instigated by Laila.

We were at supper, which like all our meals was confined to the males, plus Laila as the only female in the family young enough to eat with us, an interesting reversal of the tradition in the West where only the older children were allowed to eat with the grownups. As for the adult females, their role in the food chain seemed to be all production and no consumption. Although I often saw them preparing the food, I never once saw them eating it. Maybe the only Arabs who could enjoy privacy were the women?

They could also enjoy the fact there was never any washing up to do except for the single large dish in the center of the dinner table – for there were no water glasses, no plates, or knives or forks or spoons. To drink, you took the clay water jug from the sill of the open window high up in the wall where it was kept to catch the cool breeze, tipped your head back and poured the water directly into your mouth without the spout touching your lips. To eat, you tore off a piece of a hollow slab of unleavened bread, shaped it into a ladle, and dipped it in the communal plate.

As I did just that on this occasion, Laila slapped my hand, "*Shaitan*! Only the Devil uses his left hand."

I asked what was wrong with my left hand, I'd washed both hands before supper.

Under his breath, Ahmed explained that God had intended a man's left hand to be used for only two things: cleaning himself after using a lavatory and touching women.

It was true that the concept of toilet paper had apparently never really caught on in the traditional Middle East, where instead of sitting on a throne, you squatted over a hole in the floor, and then used your left hand to clean yourself with water from the adjacent tap. So there was a genuine need to wash this hand pretty thoroughly afterwards. But in equating excrement with women Islam seemed to be going a bit far, given the otherwise almost exaggerated respect with which it treated the female sex.

As always, Abd al-Haqq put me straight: the taboo on touching women was related to ancient menstrual prescriptions that were common to all three of the great Middle East religions. We had the chauvinism of grandpa Abraham to thank for that. It certainly wasn't just Islam, read Leviticus:

> *And if a woman have an issue and her issue in her flesh be blood, she shall be put apart seven days and whosoever toucheth her shall be unclean until the even and every thing that she lieth upon in her separation shall be unclean.*

In the Abrahamic religions, menstruating women were classed with the other 'abominations', said Abd al-Haqq. He went on to explain that according to the Old Testament, the only way you were going to get through life was to be blessed by God; to be blessed you had to be holy, to be holy you had to be whole, to be one – just like God. So above all else, you had to strive for unity, integrity, perfection, and to preserve this you had to preserve the order of creation. Anything that upset that order was an abomination, impure, unclean. Since the early Israelites were pastoralists, cloven-hooved, cud-chewing ungulates were their model of the proper kind of food. Hares and badgers broke the rule because although they appeared to be ruminants, they didn't have cloven hooves, so you couldn't eat them. Pigs broke the rule the other the way round because although they had cloven hooves, they didn't chew the cud.

"So that's why pigs aren't kosher?" I asked. "Not

because they won't keep in hot weather or because the Canaanites used to worship them?"

"Exactly," responded Abd al-Haqq, "the same applied to flying creatures with four legs and swimming creatures without scales or fins – and to women who were having their period. None of them fitted the divine pattern, so they were all unclean."

"But why are we meant to touch excrement and women with our *left* hands? Why is left bad and right good?"

"Read the *Talmud*," said the Slave of Truth, "one of the names for Satan is *Samael*, which is related to *se'mol*, the Hebrew word for 'the left side.' But Muslims were hardly the only ones to be suspicious of the left. Even in your oh-so-sophisticated Western world, it has a pretty bad reputation, from communist conspirators to courts of law. Try raising your left hand next time you take a legal oath and see how far you get."

12

Some people had fairies at the bottom of their garden. The Haidamis had Jesus; Gordon's Tomb to be precise, aka the Garden Tomb, the place amateur archaeologist General Charles Gordon believed he had established definitively as the site where Jesus was buried by Joseph of Arimathea. It was supposed to have been a family vault set just below "Skull Hill", or Golgotha, where Christ was crucified.

It spite of all the enforced Bible study and the hours of boredom I'd spent in school chapel, the image that always came to mind when my family talked of this tomb, was not of the Son of God, but of Gordon himself. Specifically, the 19th century painting – perhaps the world's most famous image of colonialism in action – which showed the great man, moments before his heroic death, standing alone at the top of a flight of steps in Khartoum facing down a horde of turbaned Islamic fuzzy-wuzzies, who are threatening him with their spears. He is holding out one arm bent at the elbow in a parrying motion, but not in fear, God no, Heaven forbid, more as if he is saying, "Oh dear, what absolutely frightful people!"

That was my heritage, the archetypal image of my race, the race that had shouldered the White Man's Burden to go out and conquer the wogs.

Well, now I was one of the wogs, one of the "wily oriental gentlemen." For nothing gave me more pleasure than to dress up as an Arab in the traditional floor-length robe and red and white checkered headscarf. Along with Ahmed, who would also don the traditional Palestinian togs for the occasion, I would then go to lean over the fence that separated the bottom of our garden from the famous tomb to toy with the pot-bellied American tourists who were eagerly clambering all over Calvary.

Like flies to a honey pot, these Michelin men would charge over to the fence, spilling out of their Bermuda shorts in their haste to take a picture of us natives with our ready supply of mother-of-pearl Domes of the Rock and knock-off olive wood crucifixes.

Now was the time for me to exercise my haggling

skills. It was like taking candy from a baby. Finally, I could empathize with the merchants of the *souq* who felt so let down by foreign customers who didn't know the rules of the game.

Ahmed and I would chatter away in Arabic, interspersed with bursts of excruciatingly broken English, extras in a B movie about the Sheikh of Araby.

Sooner or later, one of the tourists would remark on my blue eyes.

I would lean close to them with a wink and mutter darkly: "Those Crusaders, you know, they left their mark."

The Bermuda Shorts would chortle; they couldn't wait to get back to Idaho to tell that one to the neighbors.

13

Damascus gate. How many images did *that* conjure up? All the way from Saul leaving Jerusalem on his way to Damascus to become Paul, to Saladin reconquering the city from the Crusaders, to Suleiman the Magnificent re-building it and finally to General Allenby swaggering through it at the end of the Great War. But to me it was simply the gate to the Old City across the road from the Haidamis that I liked to run through with my friends.

Turn left as as you go through the gate and you hit the Via Dolorosa and the Dome of the Rock, turn right and you hit the *souq*. And it was the *souq* that interested us most, especially when we were running, which seemed to be most of the time. When your love life is confined to a few moments of eye contact once a week across a crowded cinema lobby, you have a great deal of testosterone to burn. Although my friends lived like monks, it was funny that in stark contrast with what so many young men got up to in English boarding schools, I never saw the slightest sign of any "queer" stuff among them. And as for solitary sex, well that would require solitude wouldn't it?

So we ran a lot. *Yallah, yallah, yallah,* we would cry, the equivalent of "let's go by God" as we leapt with dream-like recklessness over the mounds of melons and pomegranates and erotic spices, darting in and out of the tiny shops, continually trying to trip each other up, and generally making complete nuisances of ourselves as the sights and sounds and perfumes of three thousand years of history streamed by us like water off a duck's back. We just kept running and running. What else could you do in a society that appeared to be set set up to keep everyone a virgin, from Mary on down?

Every few weeks, we would pause in one of our headlong dashes through the Old City to stop in a small barber's shop where one of Ahmed's innumerable "cousins" would rapidly knit together a cat's cradle of black thread, and carefully snip off my facial hairs in a swift scissors-like movement as he alternately tightened and loosened the mesh of thread.

Sometimes I had a shirt ironed. The barber would dampen the shirt by taking in a mouthful of water and then spraying it evenly all across the material through his pursed lips, moving his head from side to side like a lawn sprinkler as he worked out the wrinkles with the hot iron. It reminded me of rubbing your head and your stomach at the same time – only I knew these same precise movements had been repeated unchanged for millennia.

On another occasion, I ran a little too fast and fell and cut my leg. Ibrahim picked me up like a pillow case of laundry and ran with me down a side street to a medical clinic that was as up-to-date as the barber's shop was antediluvian. In spite of the fact that there were a dozen or more patients waiting to see the doctor, I was immediately jumped to the head of the queue where my wound was treated with quiet efficiency. None of the other patients seemed to mind in the least.

The doctor asked me to come back every day for treatment, and when I got better to come back anyway, just to talk.

It goes without saying that I was never allowed to pay for any of this. Any more than I was allowed to pay for the surprise they had in store for me to make up for my fall.

I'd smoked a hubble-bubble before, but what they offered in the café they now took me to was quite different. This was better than going to the pub. Much better, I giggled. What was this stuff bubbling up through the rose water? Best tobacco I'd ever bubbled.

Through their own giggles, my friends explained that it wasn't tobacco, it was *hashish*.

What a lovely word, I thought, and giggled some more. What did it mean?

"Grass," Abd al-Haqq, struggling to keep a straight face.

What a lovely bubbly word *hashish* was, I thought again. The combination of the hard breathy "h" and the "shsh" really did sound like wind blowing through tall grass.

I remarked that I had no idea you could smoke your front lawn expecting a laugh at this clever turn of phrase.

"Not *that* grass," groaned Abd al-Haqq, rolling his eyes.

Finally, the piasta dropped.

"Oh, you mean marijuana?"

"Yes," he said, making a fierce face now, "and the people who smoke it are called the *Hashishin.* That's where we get the word 'Assassins'."

He told me of the Islamic sect back in Crusader days who believed it was their religious duty to murder their enemies. They'd lived up in the Syrian hills under the command of *As-Sheikh al-Jabal*, "The Old Man of the Mountain." To get up courage before setting out to wreck mayhem, they had smoked *hashish*, which induced ecstatic visions of paradise to get them in the mood for martyrdom.

"Seventy virgins and all that?" I said, remembering what the *Qur'an* said about paradise. I giggled again. "So shall we go out and assassinate someone?"

Abd al-Haqq suddenly went deadly serious, "It's no laughing matter."

14

It was ear-splitting. All the women in the neighborhood were standing outside the Haidami house *ululating* their heads off, their tongues flapping up and down in their mouths like frightened birds caught in a jam jar as they howled and moaned and rocked their bodies to and fro. Had the world come to an end? Were we all about to be murdered in our beds? Was the universe finally imploding on itself back into nothingness? No, it was simply that Noor Haidami was getting married to Ayyub Saeed.

A few weeks ago, Mr. and Mrs. Saeed had decided it was time for their son to take a wife. They'd gone to visit all their friends to look over the daughters of each household and report back their findings to Ayyub. After agreeing with him on the most favorable evaluation – the major criteria being that she was a good worker and a good cook, as opposed to being a fragile, useless beauty – they had then taken Ayyub to visit the girl in question: Noor Haidami. Over a timid cup of coffee, the two had eyed each other discreetly. Since neither perceived any obvious blemishes in the other, the marriage arrangements could begin.

The first step in this process was now taking place. At five o'clock on the dot, the Sheikh had arrived at the Haidami house. He was a very old, very dignified and very noble-looking man in a fawn robe over a white tunic and white shoes, with a red tarboosh wrapped in white cloth on his head. Ibraham, who along with all my other Jerusalem friends was on the invitation list, whispered to me that the Sheikh only wore the cylindrical hat because it was the perfect shape to hide his bottle of arak.

All the males of the two families and their friends sat in the "front parlor" as the Sheikh "wrote the book", which consisted of entering the details of the marriage in a register, while all the females sat outside in the garden. There was an air of friendly formality, with coffee, lemonade, chocolate and cigarettes, as the older men fingered their prayer beads and mumbled Koranic verses in the background. One of the most honored of the male guests was the laborer who worked in the flourmill next door to the Haidamis; a perfect example of Islamic socialism in action.

Next, the Sheikh summoned everyone, male and female, to pray and we all recited the *Fatiha*, the opening verse of the Koran, with our hands held out in front of us, palms up.

> *In the name of God, the Merciful, the*
> *Compassionate*
> *Praise belongs to God, the Lord of all Being,*
> *the All-merciful, the All-compassionate,*
> *the Master of the Day of Doom.*
> *Thee only we serve; to Thee alone we pray*
> *for succor. Guide us in the straight path, the*
> *path of those whom Thou hast blessed, not*
> *of those against whom Thou art wrathful,*
> *nor of those who are astray.*

We then used our hands to mime washing our faces.

This was followed by the Sheikh leading the bridegroom in the recitation of more verses from the Koran. After which, Ayyub paid Mrs. Haidami his dowry for Noor, the equivalent of about £100, and we all shook hands and said *mabrook* – congratulations.

Finally, all the women of the neighborhood, who were now gathered outside the house, began to express their joy by means of yet more of the *ululating* that had so alarmed me at first.

The writing of the book made the happy pair almost as good as married. They would now be able to enjoy the extraordinary privilege of going to the cinema or the café alone together, without a chaperone. But they wouldn't be fully married until they moved into their new house where they would finally be permitted to consummate their union. After that momentous event, there would be another more elaborate party and their engagement rings would be shifted from the right to the left hand.

I didn't even need to resort to the wisdom of Abd al-Haqq on this one. It was a no-brainer as the Americans say. Such absurdly cold and calculating and archaic marriage arrangements couldn't possibly work. Our Western ways were obviously infinitely superior resulting in our sky high divorce rate as compared to the Arab rate, which hovered around zero.

15

The stampede at the airport as I was about to take off for England was even more raucous than the ululating women at Noor's wedding. At least, it looked like a stampede to me. Ever since I'd arrived in Jerusalem, I've been surrounded by a group of young Arabs, but in some parts of Palestine such groups had grown into a large crowd.

On one occasion, my brothers had taken me to the town of *al-Khalil* – "the friend" – also known as Hebron from the Hebrew for *chaver*, so-called because Abraham the "friend of God" had stopped there. My Jerusalem buddies had prepared me in advance by explaining that the *Khalilis* were a race apart: simple-minded folk who had somehow managed to remain isolated from the rest of humanity. This made them the butt of numerous jokes. If the English had the Irish to poke fun at, the French the Corsicans, and the Canadians the Newfies, the Palestinians had the Khalilis.

So I wasn't that surprised by the looks of slack-jawed bewilderment that greeted me as my friends and I walked down the streets of Hebron. I might as well have been from Mars. But what really took me aback was that every one of the round-eyed locals immediately fell in step behind me like so many children following the Pied Piper. What tune was I subconsciously playing for them?

Now as I waited for my plane it looked as if not only half the Old City of Jerusalem and – touchingly – a number of people from the Bethlehem refugee camp (God knows how they'd afforded the bus fare), but quite a few Khalilis had gathered to wave goodbye and wish for me to go in peace: *ma'a Salaam* No airport in the West would have permitted such a mob of people to climb across its counter, knock over its benches and generally raise such merry hell in their fight to press their noses against the departure gate. But here it was all perfectly normal. If anything, the airport ground staff appeared to be egging them on.

If there'd been backslapping and cheek kissing before, it was nothing compared to the gauntlet of hands and lips that I now had to run.

Thanks to Ibrahim the born bouncer, I escaped being completely battered to death as Abd al-Haqq, Mahmud, Farid and dear old Ahmed carrying Laila on his shoulders like some Palestinian Tiny Tim, along with the newlyweds Noor and Ayyub, managed to squeeze their way close to the ramp. Even Mrs. Haidami stood shyly by, peeping at me from under her veil.

Laila held out her little fist, asking me to guess what was in it. I gave up. She opened her hand to reveal a sesame seed biscuit.

To cover my confusion, I reached into my carry-on bag and handed her a pair of sandals.

The rest of the family immediately started to raise the usual objections. I looked into their eyes, and for the one and only time managed to stare them down.

Laila stood on tiptoe to whisper a thousand thank you's into my ear – and then, her big dark eyes glistening, she asked me to stay with her forever.

I looked down at my ticket for a long moment. As if they belonged to somebody else, through the mist I watched my hands start to rip the ticket in half.

"Excuse me, sir, that's our job," said a stewardess,

as she hurriedly took the ticket from me to tear off its main portion and return the stub.

As I walked down the ramp, a rhythmic banging of feet and hands and snapping of straightened fingers began building behind me like an orchestra of Chinese firecrackers.

"*Yallah, yallah, Abu Bassam, yalla, yallah, Abu Bassam.*"

16

Flying back over the Judean hills laid out the political landscape of what I'd been experiencing at ground level throughout my Middle Eastern summer. The length of my stay may not have been great, but the experience had been of immeasurable depth, filling me with an intense love for my hosts and a growing bitterness towards the people who had stolen their land. The view through the airplane window only reinforced these feelings as I surveyed the thin slice of this Holy Land that was all that remained to the Palestinians as they sat cheek by jowl with the great sprawling indignity of modern Israel.

On the Palestinian side, it really was their land of milk and honey, for honey was the color of the hills, and honey-yellow and milky-white were the colors of the limestone Arab dwellings that grew organically out of the ancient rock framed by the brilliant blue sky. Modesty was the operative word, from modesty of dress and speech to the modesty of the traditional Arab houses, small unassuming cubes with tiny windows, as if striving to make as quiet an urban statement as possible. This was matched by the traditional Arab robes still worn by the older men and nearly all the women, in perfect harmony with the prophetic landscape.

The robes themselves told a story. When the very way you speak and write is fixed in time, and the very grammar of your life is forever suspended like an insect in amber, there's no such thing as change. The way most Arabs dressed even today was exactly the same as it was in Biblical times. It was yet another irony that the cute little Christmas crèches displayed every December in Western shopping malls brimming with the latest designer outfits featured characters dressed in robes that hadn't altered one stitch in two thousand years. Archetypal clothes that were always in fashion, precisely because there was no fashion, because there was no change. We might mock these backward towel heads for the rest of the year, but during our most important Christian festival we worshipped them.

The Israeli side of the great divide, in contrast, was a veritable slave to fashion, a celebration of incessant change and flagrant immodesty. It was as if these largely Western immigrants had gone out of their way to build their gleaming shopping malls and soaring office towers from the most outlandish materials they could find, from sheet glass and reinforced concrete to chrome and stainless steel. The "fuck-you" school of architecture, cocking a snoot not only at the original inhabitants of the land, but at the very land itself. And all of this was perfectly complemented by the exhibitionism of so many of the Israeli women in their

2

I felt about six inches high. If reading Arabic was like falling down a rabbit hole back into the seventh century, riding around in this British Embassy Mercedes on my first tour of Cairo was like taking a swig of Alice's shrinking medicine, making me feel smaller and smaller at every turn of the wheel. My driver, Neema, was a pretty young Egyptian diplomat in expensive clothes from Paris, who apparently spoke every known language and had read every book in print. She also knew the detailed history of every building in the city and was structuring our tour as if taking me down a never-ending series of floors in an historical department store.

We started off on the top floor, so to speak: a spanking-new government building erected by Nasser, then down on past a hotel from the British period, a French counting house from Napoleonic times, then a 16th century Ottoman mosque; further down still, a series of architectural wonders from various Arab dynasties, hearking back another seven or eight hundred years, and down and down past Roman ruins overlaying remnants of Greek conquest from Alexander's day, an excavation of the foundations of a temple from the Persian period, a dig for Assyrian relics from 600 and something B.C. I was breathless with civilization. And we hadn't even reached the basement where the Pharoahs were embalmed.

In Europe, I was used to feeling a positive cultural giant when I took wide-eyed visitors from Nebraska on tours of medieval London. But all that seemed like paddling about in a shallow ditch compared with the cultivated canyons we were now rappelling down. Now *I* was the gaping bumpkin from the "New" World.

To the freshly minted Second Secretary, Commercial Section of her Majesty's Embassy, Cairo, I felt even more American that night when Neema took me dancing at the Nile Hilton. If the London Hilton was a little island of Yanks in a sea of Limeys, this was Yankeedom with knobs on. Gold knobs, by the look of it, gold everything actually, with super-dooper, beebop-alula, over-the-top Las Vegas glitz assaulting our senses: disco lighting, transparent dance floors, fluorescent suits, mini skirts and hot-dog menus with caviar prices.

In one day, I had gone from the beginning of civilization to what would probably be the end of it.

Neema took it in all in her stride. When you've grown up with 6,000 years of history that doesn't feel like history, more like a multi-layered present – wall-to-wall Dunne time escalators, all marching in sync, an ephemeral bubble of American vulgarity wasn't going to make much difference. Might as well enjoy it before someone pricked it. So we did.

When it came time to top off the tipsy evening of groping each other to slow-motion Country and Western tunes in the expected manner, it was Neema's turn to have a swig of Alice's medicine bottle.

As we drew up outside my foreign office issue villa, this ancient soul who seemed to encompass all of time and space and to have not only seen it all but done it tradition of objectivity."

"I know. That's what I like about it."

"Well, it has come to our attention that the people on the list you prepared are not objective."

I scanned the list. "These are all Arabists, highly respected experts in the language and the culture."

"Exactly. They are hardly objective."

"I dispute that, but even if they weren't objective, if we bring any of them on board, we'll balance them with the same number of Jewish and Israeli scholars."

"I'm afraid that's not good enough."

So that was it. "Have you been talking to *B'nai Brith*?"

He handed me a second list. "These people are also all Arabists."

I glanced at the names. "Yes, but they are all also Jewish or Israeli."

"Yes, so they can give you both sides."

"But this is – "

"I'm afraid you either go with this list or we'll have to cancel the series."

"You're joking."

"Listen, David, you know as well as I do that a great deal of the funding for this television network comes from the federal government, which is at serious risk of being sued by *B'nai Brith* if we rock the boat. They can force the government to close us down – "

"I don't believe this!"

"And there's just one other condition..."

"I can hardly wait."

"We must avoid using the word 'Palestine' at any

point in the series. As you know, no state of Palestine ever actually existed and – "

But I had already slammed the door behind me.

5

Palestine. The word you couldn't use. Was it the last dirty word left in the world, now that you could hear the good old Anglo-Saxon trio: cunt, shit and fuck on television? For centuries to express these things you had to use Latin-derived words – vagina, excrement and copulate, or even worse, "have intercourse", as if it was something you did between the main dish and dessert. It was a hangover from the Norman Conquest of 1066, the one date every English schoolboy could remember. For it was from this fateful date forward that the Latin-derived French words the new ruling class from Normandy used for everyday things – *mouton* (mutton), *porc* (pork), and *boeuf* (beef) – were to be used for *food-on-the-plate*, replacing their Anglo-Saxon equivalents – sheep, pig and cow. These nasty lower-class words were now relegated to *food-on-the-hoof*, down and dirty with the bloody, muddy peasants who actually raised the poor fucking, shitty cunts.

But now there had been a linguistic revolution and the descendants of the Anglo-Saxon peasants had dredged their short, sharp monosyllables out of the farmyard dung and back into the light of day after a thousand years of repression by the Latin-lovers. The dirty words had come clean.

But "Palestine" was still dirty. It didn't sound dirty;

themselves in the Holy Land.

Nothing wrong with that on the face of it, except that the film climaxed, as it said in the press release, "in the struggle of the infant nation to survive attacks from its Middle Eastern enemies." So much for the Palestinian side of the story. What hope was there of ever hearing that at the movies? Well, who made the movies? Every single one of the original Hollywood studios was founded by people who came from an almost identical background: they were all Eastern European Jewish immigrants: Adam Zuckor and Jesse Lasky (Paramount), Carl Laemmle (Universal), William Fox (20th Century Fox), Samuel Goldwyn and Louis B. Mayer (MGM), Harry Cohn (Columbia) and Benjamin Warner (Warner Brothers).

And there was nothing wrong with that either, on the face of it. This particular group of Jews had a unique gift for storytelling that had gone on to dominate the world's imagination. Their very DNA seemed to spiral around a type of universal human narrative that was founded on hope and a happy ending – and if there was ever a people who deserved a happy ending surely it was the Jews!

Prior to the establishment of this southern Californian "empire of their own" as it had been described, drama had traditionally had only two faces, as witnessed with the classical Greek sad/happy mask representing tragedy and comedy. Tragedies ended tragically and comedies ended happily – until the movie-making Jewish immigrants' radical new idea of a "Hollywood ending" for every drama, tragic or comic came along.

And this was just fine by me – who wanted his movie theater exodus to be on a down note? Except for one thing: could the fact that the ethnic makeup of Hollywood was almost entirely Jewish, from its founders some eighty years ago to today's distributors, theater chain owners, publicists, producers, directors, writers, executives, managers and agents, possibly be a clue to why, although there have been literally hundreds of pro-Israel propaganda movies, there had never been a single production that showed the Palestinian point of view?

American television too, had long had an equally Jewish flavor, particularly TV comedy; it was literally a Who's Who of funny men and women, all from the same ethnic background. It had started in silent movie days with such legends as the Marx Brothers and the Three Stooges leading to Woody Allen, Jack Benny, Milton Berle, Mel Brooks, George Burns, Sid Caesar, Jerry Lewis, Gene Wilder, and running all the way to the days of Roseanne Barr, David Brenner, Billy Crystal, Goldie Horn, Madeline Kahn, Adam Sandler, Jerry Seinfeld, Garry Shandling and Jon Stewart, the list went on and on. These comics as well as the preponderantly Jewish writers who wrote their hilarious lines all seem to have imbibed a Catskillian rhythm and pacing with their mothers' milk. The familiar one-two-three-punch-line cadence of the sitcoms, with the machine-generated laugh track every fifteen seconds was pure Borscht Belt. Even the late-night TV talk shows followed this rimshot rhythm: the

the Beast as recorded in the good old Book of Revelation 13:18. Your guess is as good as mine.

But at least the meetings in Cairo and Kuwait had gone well and the necessary funds had come together. There was only one, quite understandable, condition: I had to secure television distribution in North America.

So, armed with story outlines for all twelve one-hour episodes, plus an ironclad guarantee of funding, I sent off letters to all the major television networks in North America. Here was a series showing a world that we must understand, whatever side we're on. It would be produced in both English and Arabic, thereby almost doubling the potential audience, and on top of that it wouldn't cost the networks a dime. Surely this was an offer even the most dedicated Israeli flag-waving television executive couldn't refuse?

The terse replies might all have been written by the same person and boiled down to one sentence: we are not interested in broadcasting propaganda.

7

They were all cowards wrote "Disgusted Tunbridge Wells", "Appalled East Cheam" and "Outraged Sunbury-on-Thames" to the newspapers, reacting to another spate of suicide bombing in Israel. But was it really so cowardly to be a suicide bomber? What would any of us do in their place? You've lost your history, your country, your home, along with almost all of your relatives and friends, and you cannot travel outside of the miserable ghetto you share with God know how many other pariahs. You have no medicine, hardly any food, and your water and your air is polluted as you watch your children slowly die. Every day your head throbs with the ear-splitting roar of giant fighter planes and gunships circling overhead looking for new targets for their missiles and bullets. Every day another pathetic shack is bulldozed and flattened into a mini-moonscape of rubble and dust, whether or not anyone is living in it. Every day there is a new humiliation at the hands of squads of soldiers hardly more than teenagers, calling you every filthy name under the sun. You have no education, no job, no hope, no future, no life.

What exactly was this hopeless, helpless, despairing people living on forty cents a day meant to do? It was already clear what would happen if they did nothing, they would become nothing themselves. The Israeli settlement-building machine had already planted nearly half a million settlers in the West Bank squeezing the Palestinians into ever smaller pockets of misery, setting up over 600 checkpoints that forced them to line up for hours just to get to the next village.

The 1967 war had resulted in Israel expanding its territory to cover 78% of Palestine, leaving the Palestinians with 22%.

Right up to the present day, Israel had never ceased grabbing more and more of the choice bits of the West Bank for its more than one million "settlers," until only about 40% of the 22% – i.e., 8.8% – remained to the

Palestinians. And even this measly bit of Palestine was to be chopped up into tiny isolated fragments of the worst land, where the Palestinians were barely surviving in some of the most appalling conditions anywhere on the planet.

It was like *The Pit and the Pendulum* squeezing the prisoner into a smaller and smaller space until there was no longer an inch of foothold. "I struggled no more, but the agony of my soul found vent in one loud, long, and final scream of despair."

As you totter on the brink of nothingness, do you just avert your eyes like Poe's prisoner, or do you use the only weapon you have to fight back: your own body? Is this really such a moral stretch? Is it really so cowardly to pit your soft flesh against the iron and steel of the Apache helicopters and the F16s and the 60-ton Caterpillar bulldozers, to play David and Goliath without a slingshot? Would any of the outraged writers to the newspapers have had the courage to do this? Would I have had the courage to do this when I was a young man? When it came right down to it, would I have had what it takes to strap on the explosives and walk into the crowded street?

They called themselves martyrs. We called them terrorists. So they called us terrorists back. So we called ourselves heroes. The cretinous ritual of name-calling as infantile as a kindergarten playground and as old as the human race.

This hideous dialogue was made all the more harrowing by the fact that the word used for suicide bomber throughout the Arab world – including all of the Arab media — was *shaheed*, which had the dual meaning of "a martyr killed in battle with the infidel" and "one who bore witness to God." Bearing witness to God consisted of reciting the *shahaada* (same route as *shaheed*): *la illaha illa Allah wa Muhammad rasul Ullah*, "There is no god but God, and Muhammad is the Messenger of God." Since this was the single most sacred phrase in the world's most sacred language by the simple utterance of which you instantly became a Muslim, for a believer in Islam to criticize suicide bombing was roughly equivalent to a believer in Christianity denouncing the nicene Creed.

All of this and more was running through my mind, contrasting grotesquely with the happy state of my own personal affairs since I was finally about to realize a life-long dream: I was about to emigrate to America to make documentaries for one of the public television stations there.

For me, as for most English people growing up during after World War Two, not to mention millions of people growing up in other parts of the world, America was our great shining hope, as shiny as its twinkling, sparkling, shimmering flag crammed with such brazen quantities of stars and stripes. As a child, before the nuclear explosion of rock'n roll, hamburgers and James Dean changed all of our lives, my very first memories of America where of my collection of tiny American flags made of silk, mounted on matchstick flagpoles. I worshipped those flags, so infinitely more thrilling than the dark, stuffy Union Jacks that went with mournful ceremonies on dark November afternoons laying wreaths on cenotaphs. The American flag went with jeeps and Gis and chiclets and everything you ever wanted, just there for the asking, all bathed in brilliant, everlasting Californian sunshine.

During the war, our whole year climaxed with the Christmas fruitcakes sent over by kind Milwaukee cousins with rimless spectacles. They were stuffed with glazed oranges and lemons, cherries and raisins, and more nuts than we knew what to do with, with only the merest hint of actual cake in between. The profligracy, the generosity, the Sears catalogs the cakes were wrapped in!

So many wonders in those catalogues I never could have imagined: swing sets and snooker tables, swimming pools and putting greens. My favourites were the shiny-bright zip-up jackets. *Zip-zip*. The word was pure American. In England, you didn't zip, you laboriously buttoned damp serge. And they had no collars those daring silken jackets, just a ribbon of bright red or blue or yellow or green round the neck, thumbing their nose at the boring old lapels of our school uniforms. And then the miracle of being able to turn the jacket inside out and have a whole other jacket, with different colours all over again. It was a conjuring trick, the technicolor scarves the magician pulled out of his pocket going on forever and ever. Of course, I never actually owned one of these coats of many colours. They only existed for me as glossy paper images, but I would gloat over them for hours

And now the gloating was over, now at last I was going to get my hands on the Real Thing.

Just as life was going worse than ever for my Palestinian friends, life was going better than ever for me. What an obscene contrast between my world and theirs.

soared so very, very far above their heads.

Just to explore one instance: the vastness and richness of the Arabic language itself encompassed delicate shades of meaning and rice-paper thin distinctions between states of being to an extent no one who hadn't studied the language could possibly imagine, condensing what would be lengthy phrases in English into single words. Typical examples were *ta'abata*, "to carry under one's arm"; *tataahama*, "to get along well together"; *aq'as*, "a person with a protruding chest and a hollow back"; or *fitr,* " the space between the end of the thumb and the end of the index finger when extended."

This huge Arabic vocabulary also made it possible to express concepts that literally couldn't be *conceived* in a Western language because there was no word for them. These ranged from *mulaqqin*, "an expert in Islamic jurisprudence who instructs the deceased at his grave what to tell the two angels of death," to *ruqbaa*, "a donation that reverts to the donor after the donee's death unless the donor dies before the donee, in which case the donation becomes the permanent property of the donee and his beneficiaries after his death." (Take that, *heterobalneopote*.) Thanks to their almost bottomless treasure chest of a language, the Arabs were able to slice up thought itself into much finer morsels than speakers of Western languages.

By comparison, Indo-European speakers were linguistic snails oblivious of any thought moving too fast to be conceptualized by our limited vocabularies. Or to put it another way: it was if the Arabs had sped up their movie to honey bee speed: two hundred and fifty pictures per second, as opposed to our measly twenty-four, with the grade seven reading level of the cable newscasters slithering along at the back of the pack.

Cut to a commercial for junk food and carbonated water, a plug for underarm deodorant, and an instant cure for flaking toenails

Cut back to Chainsaw grinding her way through yet another wooden monologue. Although I had to admit there was lots of grist for her glittering chompers. The latter-day *hashisheen* were working overtime with their suicide bombings occurring so frequently and being so overreacted to by Israel's military machine that the horrors were almost becoming boring.

Tit for tat, yelled the children, you bomb me and I'll bomb you back ten times more. Oh yeah? Then I'll bomb you back a hundred times more. Oh yeah? Then I'll... and on and on it went, the lunatic escalation beating its head into a pulp again and again against the same blood-stained wall dividing the two sons (and daughters) of Shem.

But now the TV jockeys – Chainsaw had been joined by the usual silver-haired male co-host old enough to be her grandfather – seemed to have regained some of their initial enthusiasm for the subject, because this time it was different. This time it wasn't a young man but a middle-aged woman who had strapped on the explosives. And even our genial hosts had to admit she'd had rather a rough life.

They breezed through the details as fast as they

could of course, but even they couldn't completely sanitize the fact that her father had been shot by the Israelis when she was a baby. Years later, she herself had been beaten and repeatedly raped by renegade Israeli soldiers along with her mother and older sister while her three brothers were forced to watch before they had their testicles burned off with cigarettes and were carted away to spend the rest of their lives in prison as the Haidamis' Jerusalem house was razed to the ground.

But of course incomparably more important than that was the Israeli side of the equation, for the female terrorist's victim happened to have been a Tel Aviv woman of almost exactly the same age and appearance. They showed pictures of the dead pair side by side: the Palestinian and the Israeli, evil versus good, two worlds collide, blah blah blah, "East is East and West is West and never the twain shall meet", said Kipling, over a hundred years ago. Nothing had changed.

But they could have been sisters: recent photos showing both of them in their mid-forties, both still very pretty with their deep black eyes staring earnestly into the camera.

One of them looked strangely familiar. I squinted at the name on the screen: Laila Haidami.

2

As I stared blankly at the TV know-it-alls who were now glibly explaining away the latest Israeli bulldozing and bombing of tens of thousands of women and children in Gaza as "self-defense", I tried to imagine what little Laila had gone through.

Had she raised her arms at the critical moment as recommended in the martyrdom manuals so as to maximize the damage and turn himself into a human cluster bomb? My little angel of death trying her wings. I'd seen TV clips from some Hamas terror camp's rows of suicide vests hanging up in neat plastic wrappers like so many team sweaters waiting to be picked up at the dry cleaners by a busy soccer mom. But these vests were studded with explosives and ball bearings and weighed thirty pounds, a lot for my little Laila. The old Mae West joke "Is that a gun in your pocket or are you just pleased to see me?" had flipped into "Are those pomegranates under your blouse for me or are they just hand grenades?"

I thought back to our "last supper" in Jerusalem all those years ago.

In my honor, we were enjoying my favorite Palestinian meal of all: *Mulukhia*, a dark green soup made from the vegetable known as "Jew's mallow", thick enough to be scooped up in a fold of bread. This to be followed by my second favorite dish: *Waraq al-anab al-mahshi*, vine leaves stuffed with rice and lamb.

"*Bisihhaticum*", I had said, as I drank to the health of Ahmed, Mahmud, Farid and their special guest, Abd al-Haqq. I said it as loudly as I could for the benefit of Mrs. Haidami and Nour confined as usual to the kitchen, the door of which had been left ajar in honor of the occasion. Although trying to make a toast when you've only got one water jug between you was a bit like trying to clap with one hand, but you did your best.

"*Ana uhibbak*, Abu Bassam," said Laila, echoing Jasmine. I looked once again into her midnight eyes which always reminded me of the Arabic word *ahwar* meaning the contrast between the black of the cornea and the black of the iris, which was also cognate with *houriah*, or houri, a "virgin of paradise."

I couldn't help wondering yet again that if suicide-bombing males were rewarded with seventy-two such virgins, what were suicide-bombing virgins rewarded with?

I knew what little Laila had always wanted – from me, anyway – it was to tell her the story, always the same story, the one about American cowboys. She settled down in my lap as I returned – for what was to prove to be one last time – to the Wild West.

When it was over, she kissed me and said, *Ana majnunah*", literally, "I am possessed by a jinn or genie", "mad", in other words, only in this context, "I am mad with love for you."

The Virgin of Paradise then promptly fell asleep.

I remarked to my companions that it was hard to hear talk of romantic love in a world where women were set apart as unattainable objects, hidden behind veils and the walls of harems.

Yet again, I was quietly corrected, this time by Ahmed, who said it was precisely this sequestering of women which had given birth to the idea of romantic love in the first place.

The four young men then took turns in recounting

the ancient tale of the tragic love affair of *Qays wa Laila*, who came from two rival clans and who were to inspire Shakespeare's *Romeo and Juliet*. Qays fell so madly in love with Laila that people called him insane – *majnun* – and the story itself was often referred to as *Majnun wa Laila*.

"You know," said Abd al-Haqq, "the whole idea of worshipping the lady in the tower, the whole cult of courtly love was actually picked up from us by the Crusaders. You Europeans had no tradition of passionate or romantic love literature, any more than did the Greeks or the Romans, who thought passionate love was either a punishment inflicted by the gods, or just sensual gratification, not to be taken seriously. You couldn't have the passion – the 'madness' – without the veils and the high walls and ending your Arabic letters with 'May the nightingale forever sing at the bottom of your garden,' which rather puts 'Yours sincerely' in the shade, doesn't it?"

Enough, I thought, it was time to get my own back by showing them a card trick I was rather proud of. I produced a pack of playing cards from my rucksack. Here's something I can teach you that comes from the Western world."

They all burst out laughing. Damn, had I made yet another gaffe in Arabic?

"Don't you know where playing cards come from?" said Abd al-Haqq.

"Let me guess," I said, closing my eyes.

"Just one more cultural treasure plundered by your Crusaders," said the relentless Slave of Truth. In fact, one particular group of Crusaders used to be on the cards themselves. Originally there were four Kings, four Queens, four Knaves, and four *Knights*."

"Really?" He'd got me again.

"Remember the day we visited the Dome of the Rock?"

"I certainly did: a permanent sunrise popping up right smack in the middle of the Old City. When the Muezzin called, it was the ultimate *Son et Lumière*.

"Well, the early Muslims deliberately built the Dome on top of Solomon's Temple, one of the holiest places not only to the Jews but also to the Christians. When the Crusaders invaded Jerusalem they thought that the Dome *was* Solomon's Temple and they delegated one group of knights to guard it: the 'Knight Templars'. But these Templars were the poorest of all the knights, beggars almost – until they discovered something of unbelievable importance buried beneath the Temple, some sort of secret treasure. And all of a sudden, the big shots of Europe began donating their estates and huge sums of money to these poor knights, who became incredibly rich and powerful. So much so, that in their honor, we added a set of four knights to our playing cards."

I looked down at my cards. "So where did they go?"

"They fell foul of the Pope. They were too successful for their own good, and the Pope – the most powerful man in the world at the time – felt so threatened that he accused them of heresy, of sodomy and all sorts of other terrible blasphemies, and had them all burned at the stake. He wiped almost all trace of them off the face of the earth – including the knights in your version of the playing cards."

"So we're four short?" I said.

"Uhuh," smiled Abd al-Haqq, who'd obviously been building up to this moment. "We always said you Westerners weren't playing with a full deck!"

"Very funny," I said, "but have you Arabs got a full deck?"

"Oh yes, we preserved the four knights in what you call the Tarot cards."

"Is there anything you guys didn't invent?"

"Yep, the atom bomb for one thing."

"Oh, shut up. But seriously, was it literally the end of the Templars?"

"It seems that a few did escape to Scotland, where they went underground and disappeared with their secret treasure. Four hundred years later they re-emerged under a new name – the Freemasons."

"I knew some Freemasons at Cambridge. Is that the 'great secret' they claimed to be guarding all this time: the treasure of the Templars?"

"Possibly, that was certainly one hypothesis. But if it's correct, it begs an even more interesting question: what is this 'treasure'?"

This is where Ahmed joined in, saying there was one theory that made a lot of sense, but to explain it, it was his turn to fetch a pack of cards.

He returned with a Tarot set and laid out the four knights: Wands, Swords, Pentacles and Cups. He pointed to the Knight of Cups. "According to legend the cup the knight is holding represents the cup Joseph would know a Palestinian from an Argentinian, joyfully opening the new U.S. embassy with 13 minutes of sycophantic drivel.

This included the following gem: "Our strong commitment to lasting peace, a peace that overcomes the conflicts of the past in order to give our children a brighter and more boundless future. As we have seen from the protests of the last month and even today, those provoking violence are part of the problem and not part of the solution."

So stick that up your 8.8%.

Nonetheless, it was still very strange that a group of people who hitherto had so little knowledge of or sympathy for or even interest in this region should have become so obsessed by it in recent times.

Then the answer to this conundrum walked into the expensive Spanish restaurant.

I could hardly believe my eyes. It was none other than the Great Arabist himself, Sir Leonard Goldberg. Although he must have been in his eighties by now, thanks to his mind-boggling erudition, he could still pull a snow job over the best of them.

After watching an hour or so of his finally honed performance, I realized who was the *eminence grise* behind the U.S. Middle East policy, who was providing the intellectual underpinning and scholarly rationale for America's vendetta against the Arabs, the narrative storyline for the happy-ending drama that was about to be played out. Finally, there was someone who knew *exactly* what he was talking about, who really did speak all the languages and have a deep understanding of the region.

The tragedy – if you'll pardon the expression – was that with every well-turned phrase and brilliant analogy and intriguing tidbit of historical lore, Sir Leonard was betraying the very people he'd earned his towering reputation for studying these past sixty years by subtly skewing the facts in favor of Israel and to the detriment of the Arab world.

Very few westerners who didn't have direct intimate experience of the Arabs and their culture could have spotted the delicate shading and shaping of the great man's carefully worded discourse – let alone this bunch of cultural illiterates, who duly lapped up every golden word that fell from his lips.

The effect was compounded because he was of course preaching to the converted. This was the perfect scholarly cover for the Israel's imperialistic machinations, the ideal historical justification for doing just about anything they wanted to the Middle East, from preemptive strikes and regime change to cluster carpet-bombing and bunker-busting with depleted uranium warheads.

But if you were able to see through the academic sleight-of-hand, you realized that what the renowned Arabist was actually saying boiled down to this: the Arabs were primitive and tribal, ruled by their emotions, besotted by conspiracy theories and congenitally incapable of civilized, democratic behavior.

The man even managed to turn the "orality" of the Arabs against them, putting his own gloss on Marshall *kindergarten so there would always be enough for everybody. At least that's what all the children were told.*

But for some mysterious reason that no one could fathom, seventy-two of the hot meals and seventy-two of the bags of toys always went to the six "special" children every day, so that they had twelve hot meals and twelve bags of toys each. Perhaps that was why they were just a teeny-weeny bit on the chubby side.

The remaining twenty-eight hot meals and twenty-eight bags of toys were divided up between the other ninety-four children. This meant there was never enough to go round, and perhaps explains why most of these children were so skinny and sick looking. It also led to lots of rather nasty squabbles.

The six special children's corner of the room was behind a glass wall. You could look in, but they couldn't look out, because their side of the glass was a mirror. When they weren't eating or playing with their toys, the six children spent most of the time looking into this mirror, admiring themselves for being the greatest and most special and freest children who had ever lived in the kindergarten.

We don't know about the greatest, most special and freest part, but they were certainly the fattest.

When they weren't fighting or scrabbling for not enough food and not enough toys, the other ninety-four children pressed their noses up against the glass wall, watching the six fat children have such a lovely time and looking more and more like balloons that might burst at any minute.

This went on for five hundred years.

Then one day, one of the skinny children found a small chink in the glass wall, and chucked a pebble through it that scratched the leg of one of the fat children, who burst into tears.

The six fat children were very shocked by this for nothing like it had ever happened before. For the very first time ever, they peeked out through the little hole in the glass wall and saw all the skinny, raggedy, multi-colored children, some of whom were clapping their hands and jumping up and down.

The six fat mainly white children looked at each other in puzzlement: why do they hate us?

No one had the slightest idea.

It's all very well to kick the rest of the world around for five hundred years, but don't sell them dangerous weapons while you're doing it, otherwise one fine day in September they're going to kick back. In other words, dearly beloved, don't give pebbles to skinny children.

And now, just to make absolutely sure the other children in the kindergarten hated us, America was on a rampage to take over the Arab world once and for all, starting with Iraq, next stop Syria, planning on blundering blindly around every corner of the world where they couldn't even read the street signs. How could the American public put up with this breathtaking stupidity and arrogance, this trashing of the beautiful dream?

Was it perhaps the nature of the television medium that now gave Americans 90% of their news? A picture can only show you what is, never what isn't. This meant not only that you couldn't show a picture of someone smoking, for example, and say "This isn't someone smoking", but also that you couldn't say concerning the same picture, "Don't do this." In other words, it wasn't just that you couldn't say no on TV, you also couldn't say no *to* TV, you could only say "yes", a great big slobbery yes to every bloody thing it felt like selling you, however useless or shoddy or fake. So we had a nation of poor TV-besotted saps buying into everything they saw on the idiot box from soap suds to sugary distortions of the "news" and treacly mythologizing of what little was left of their history. For apart from being a "yes medium", TV was a "present medium" collapsing all time gradations into the present tense, an internal electronic *now*, simultaneously reducing your attention span to that of a flea and erasing the past tense from your language. "Last week I go into this store and this girl she goes this one's cute and I go yeah this one's real cute and I buy it and I take it home."

On top of all this, the Americans had the web and the vacuity of social media. A brain dump or a garbage dump? A little bit of the former and a huge great pile of the latter, which was the perhaps the most striking thing about the WWW. There had long been platforms for intelligence – from books to lecture halls – but never such a platform for inanity; such an accumulation of gormlessness and nincompoopery had never seen the light of day. Hitherto, the very dense had confined their stupidity to a small circle of family and friends; now they had a soapbox the size of the planet.

Even the names the Americans used for the most popular activities on the web give the game away: everyone google-goggling like a village idiot at ounces of wisdom and megatons of bullshit, triviality and depravity, the sacred and the profane; *facebooking* about what you had for breakfast, *youtubing* home movies of your baby throwing up, *podcasting* the first things that come into your head, *yahooing* your last period, *blogging* your next haircut and *twitting* about anything at all, as long as it was something really, really dumb and shallow. Strange that nobody had drawn attention to the meanings of those last three gerunds. *Yahoo*: from Gulliver's Travels, a filthy, ignorant, brutish creature with disgusting habits. *Blog*: British slang for a mindless lout or oaf. *Twit*: a fool, a stupid or ineffectual person.

And by Heaven they were out in force today, were the yahoos and the blogs and the twits, side by side with the sages and the scholars, talking their big and little heads off.

The Arabs and the Americans really did represent a clash of incompatible time zones: if the Arabs had no future, increasingly the Americans had no past. With one exception to this: the belief of some seventy million evangelicals, dating their faith back to the 1700s, which maintained that the only way to mend the world was to destroy it by bringing about Armageddon in the Middle East centered on the very same temple in Jerusalem from which the Freemasons had inherited their great secret.

But were we all ready to go up in smoke simply because a gang of loony rednecks believed that the only way to bring about the Second Coming was for the Jews to reclaim the temple, and the only way to do that was for a rabbi to purify himself sufficiently to enter the place, and the only way to bring that about was to sacrifice a perfect three-year old red heifer with not a single white hair on her udders, then burn the heifer, mix her ashes with water, and sprinkle the mixture all over himself.

I wasn't making this up: it was all laid out in the *Book of Numbers*:

> *Speak to the sons of Israel that they bring you an unblemished red heifer in which there is no defect and on which a yoke has never been mounted. And you shall give it to Eleazar the priest, and it shall be brought outside the camp and be slaughtered in his presence. And Eleazar the priest shall take some of its blood with his finger and sprinkle some of its blood toward the front of the tent of meeting seven times. Then the heifer shall be burned in his sight; its hide, its*

flesh, and its blood, with its refuse, shall be burned. And the priest shall take cedar wood, hyssop, and scarlet material, and throw it into the midst of the burning heifer. The priest shall then wash his clothes and bathe his body in water, and afterward come into the camp; but the priest will be unclean until evening. The one who burns the heifer shall also wash his clothes in water and bathe his body in water, and will be unclean until evening.

Perhaps all God really wanted from us was to give Himself a good laugh.

It was absurd and tragic and very, very scary, all at the same time.

And yet and yet this was also the America that had come to the aid of my own country in two World Wars, particularly in World War Two when as Churchill had hopefully predicted, "...in God's good time, the New World, in all its power and might steps forth to the rescue and the liberation of the old." This was also the America of Thoreau and Dewey and Walt Whitman and Helen Keller and Hemingway and Martin Luther King and countless others I admired so much, not to mention the America of Louis Armstrong and Muddy Waters and T-Bone Walker and Lionel Hampton and Thelonious Monk and the host of other blues and jazz musicians I'd spent so much of my teenage years adoring.

The question kept coming back: how could the intelligent, reasonable, charming Americans that I met every day let the people who now ran the country get away with it? Were they besotted by the very dream itself, the lovely Jeffersonian vision of life and liberty and happiness with its corollary, that good old "happy ending" again, that Panglossian optimism that everything would turn out for the best in this best of all possible nations? The greatest nation, after all, that ever existed on the face of the earth, as the U.S. congressmen never tired of repeating.

You couldn't sustain this blind belief in the superiority of the American way without simultaneously believing in the inferiority of everybody else's way. Perhaps that was why the American dreamers who ran the country were so easily seduced by the Zionist dream, why they could be so callous and contemptuous of anyone who dared to challenge it, with particular disdain for the Palestinians who had dared to live for some fourteen hundred years on a land that didn't belong to them.

Underscore all this with an ingrained racism that had never really died. Of course these people had to be kept in their place, they were brown after all, a lower order of humanity, let's face it. Begin called Palestinians "two-legged vermin", Rafael Eitan preferred "drugged roaches in a bottle", while Shamir was content with "grasshoppers." Palestinians were by definition "an imminent threat" to everything Americans held dear, "a clear and present danger" justifying any preemptive strikes the Americans felt like making in order to "defend *our* country" from *our* weapons of mass destruction. Always the same sad little parade of stock clichés, the same limited grade school vocabulary that was all that was left to a people most of whom have become so linguistically challenged they needed sub-titles for even slightly accented English whether from the Middle East or Middlesborough.

Arundati Roy said of nationalism: "Flags are bits of colored cloth that governments use first to shrink-wrap people's minds and then as ceremonial shrouds to bury the dead."

The United States was shrink-wrapping itself into a black hole of ignorance and paranoia, a Manichean world of good and evil, light and darkness. You were either with us or against us. And if you were against us, if you failed to wave our particular bit of colored cloth for every new act of aggression, God would not help you, because He was on our side, not yours.

So here we go, the most powerful nation in the history of the human race, galloping backwards into the colonialist 19th century to bring peace to the world through war.

So what to do about this what to do?

French brandy and bales of Virginia tobacco and Belgian lace along the secret tunnel leading from the beach formed by the gap in the Downs, past the old country house, and finally up into the cellar of this 13th century hostelry where they exchanged their ill-gotten goods for the wool from the download sheep that was all the rage for European weavers.

The current name of the ancient pub, *The Moon In The Water*, gave away its checkered past. Legend had it that Sussex shepherds used to have a reputation for being simple-minded. One day such a shepherd saw two smugglers emerge from the pub and sink two kegs of brandy into a new nearby dewpond. "Aha!" said he to himself, "Come nightfall I'll have one of they."

That night, he returned to the pond and began fishing around with his crook. Suddenly, two excise men appeared and asked what he was doing. "Can't you see the old moon has fallen into the pond. I be a' trying to fish her out, but I can't seem to hook her no-ways."

The excise men rode off, having a good chuckle at the expense of the "silly Sussex", who meanwhile was happily rolling away his keg of Napoleon brandy.

I checked my watch. It was almost time. I looked around me. The bar was getting even more crowded and noisy as the second or third rounds of drinks kicked in. *Alhamdulillah*. All the better for sneaking down unobtrusively to the cellar as Abu Jamaal, aka Abd al-Haqq, had instructed me to do.

I picked up my duffel bag and quit the bar.

Going through the tunnel wasn't as hard as I'd

feared since it had apparently been cleaned out fairly recently. Still, it was going to be quite a slog at my age, a good half mile as I recalled, although that was all the way to the beach; I was going to turn off a few hundred yards before this.

Soon what I was burdened with seemed to weigh a ton. But it wouldn't be long now. Such a clever idea, to come all the way from East Jerusalem, Washington D.C. and Princeton to this Georgian country manor nestled in the Sussex downs. The country house that I knew so well. Thanks to MI6, I could certainly tell my fish knife from my cheese knife in this place, making it the perfect spot both for me and for this historic meeting for the signing of the "resettlement agreement": the Final Solution to the Palestinian problem.

Just as Abd al-Haqq had told me, the turn-off led straight up into the exquisite Georgian manor's wine cellar. Now to put on the contents of Laila's duffel bag before mounting the stairs to the Great Hall.

Next, to push open the door at the top of the stairs.

And there they were, the three most important men in my world: the young and lithe Prime Minister of Israel, the obese former President of the United States and the Great Arabist Himself, all staring at me as I walked through the door at the rear of the Great Hall, the front of my jacket now bulging, making my chest stick out like a pigeon.

Immediately, a quartet of thickset security men started to move towards me to block my way.

"Sir Leonard!" I called out, "So nice to see you after

all these years!"

The old man hesitated, but the bodyguards continued to close in on me.

The Prime Minister and the former President looked at each other in alarm. "What's going on?" cried the PM to a speechless POTUS.

"You must remember me, Sir Leonard," I said to the old man, "from the television network, the Middle East series."

"Mr. Stansfield. Yes, of course," replied the Famous Arabist.

The bodyguards came to a halt.

"What do you want?" continued the old man.

"This," I said, pulling the red cord out of Laila's now empty duffel bag and pressing the button.

ABOUT THE AUTHOR

With his wife, Denise Boiteau, David Stansfield has written and produced some four hundred television scripts for TVOntario in Canada (both in English and French), Canadian Pacific Rail, the Public Broadcasting Service in the U.S., the Discovery Channel, NHK, Encyclopedia Britannica, Time Life and Showtime.

David and Denise's TV productions have been translated into more than a dozen languages and have won over fifty international film and television awards, including the selection of their "The Middle East" series in the Academy Awards Best Educational Documentary category.

David graduated Summa Cum Laude from Durham University in Modern Arabic, followed by further studies and a First Class Honors degree in the same language at Cambridge University and the Sorbonne. He subsequently worked with Marshall McLuhan at the University of Toronto on a study of the different effects that the Roman, Arabic and Chinese writing systems have on the reader.

Most recently, David served as an Arabic consultant on the Netflix TV series "House of Cards."

Printed in Great Britain
by Amazon